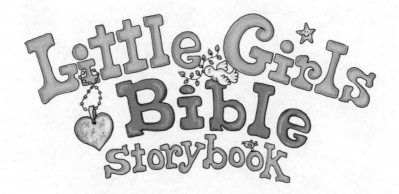

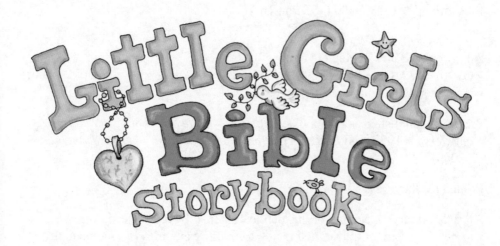

Little Girls Bible Storybook

Carolyn Larsen

Illustrated by Caron Turk

BakerBooks
Grand Rapids, Michigan

Text © 1998, 2000 by Carolyn Larsen
Illustrations © 1998, 2000 by Caron Turk

Published by Baker Books
a division of Baker Publishing Group
P.O. Box 6287, Grand Rapids, MI 49516-6287
www.bakerbooks.com

Previously published as two books: *Little Girls Bible Storybook for Mothers &
Daughters* (© 1998) and *Little Girls Bible Storybook for Fathers & Daughters*
(© 2000)

Printed in China

Library of Congress Cataloging-in-Publication Data
Larsen, Carolyn, 1950–
    Little girls Bible storybook / Carolyn Larsen ; Illustrated by Caron Turk.
       p.   cm.
    "Previously published as two books: Little girls Bible storybook for
mothers & daughters (1998) and Little girls Bible storybook for fathers &
daughters (2000)"—ECIP galley.
    ISBN 10: 0-8010-4534-7 (cloth)
    ISBN 978-0-8010-4534-9 (cloth)
    1. Bible stories, English. 2. Mothers and daughters—Religious aspects—
Christianity—Juvenile literature. 3. Fathers and daughters—Religious
aspects—Christianity—Juvenile literature. I. Turk, Caron. II. Title.
BS551.3.L373 2007
220.9′505—dc22   2007007949

Scripture is taken from the *Holy Bible*, New Living Translation, copyright ©
1996. Used by permission of Tyndale House Publishers, Inc., Wheaton, Illinois
60189. All rights reserved.

Contents

Part 2: Stories for Fathers and Daughters

Part 1

Stories
for Mothers
and Daughters

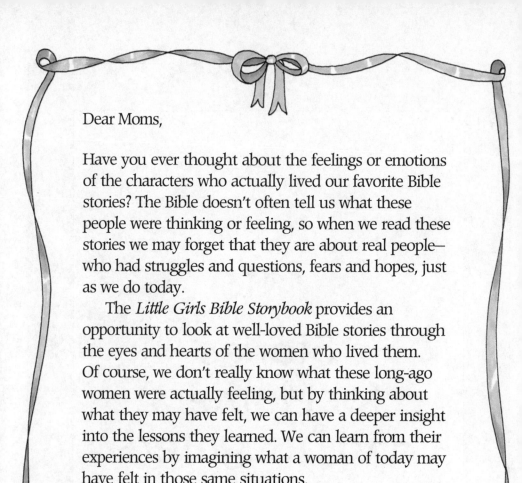

Dear Moms,

Have you ever thought about the feelings or emotions of the characters who actually lived our favorite Bible stories? The Bible doesn't often tell us what these people were thinking or feeling, so when we read these stories we may forget that they are about real people—who had struggles and questions, fears and hopes, just as we do today.

The *Little Girls Bible Storybook* provides an opportunity to look at well-loved Bible stories through the eyes and hearts of the women who lived them. Of course, we don't really know what these long-ago women were actually feeling, but by thinking about what they may have felt, we can have a deeper insight into the lessons they learned. We can learn from their experiences by imagining what a woman of today may have felt in those same situations.

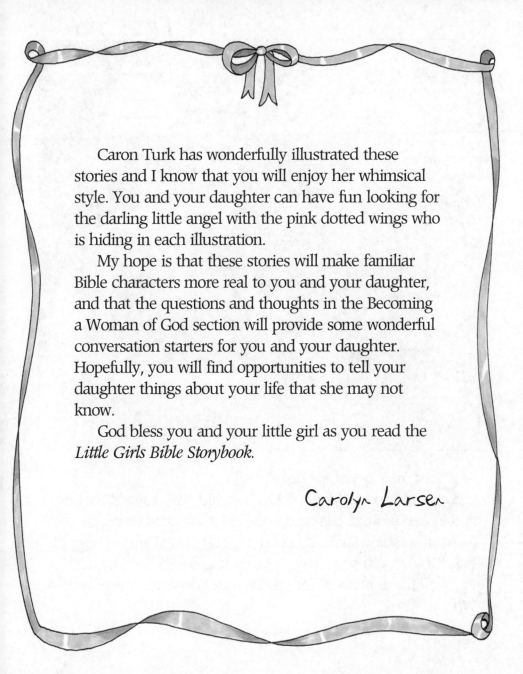

Caron Turk has wonderfully illustrated these stories and I know that you will enjoy her whimsical style. You and your daughter can have fun looking for the darling little angel with the pink dotted wings who is hiding in each illustration.

My hope is that these stories will make familiar Bible characters more real to you and your daughter, and that the questions and thoughts in the Becoming a Woman of God section will provide some wonderful conversation starters for you and your daughter. Hopefully, you will find opportunities to tell your daughter things about your life that she may not know.

God bless you and your little girl as you read the *Little Girls Bible Storybook*.

Carolyn Larsen

The First Sin

"Pssst, hey, over here, lady!"
    With juice dripping down her chin, Eve stopped eating and looked around. Seeing no one, she took another big bite. Suddenly a shiny snake dropped its head down right in front of her. "Oh my, you scared me," Eve exclaimed. "Wait a minute, I know all the animals in the garden, but I don't recognize you. Who are you?"

And the Lord God planted

the tree of knowledge...

a garden toward the east,

"Let'ssssss just sssssay I'm a friend"

in Eden...and God caused to grow

"Never mind," the snake hissed. "Why are you eating that? You could have the s-s-sweetest fruit in the garden."

"Which fruit are you talking about?" Eve asked.

"It's-s-s on that big tree in the center of the garden," the snake hissed.

"But God said not to eat that fruit," said Eve.

"Trus-s-st me, it's-s-s-s the s-s-s-sweetest, run-down-your-chin juiciest fruit in the whole garden."

"You make it sound so good," Eve whined.

"God didn't really mean that you s-s-shouldn't eat that fruit." The snake wrapped his body around Eve's shoulders like an old friend.

"B-b-but," Eve started to argue, but the snake led her to the big beautiful tree.

"Come on, try it!"

Eve looked at the fruit, then at the snake. Suddenly she grabbed the fruit and bit into it.

the serpent was a crafty beast.....

This was a sad day for Adam and Eve

"Adam, try this!" Eve called. "It's the yummiest."

"That fruit is from the tree God told us to stay away from," Adam shouted. But he couldn't resist taking a bite of it, too.

Adam and Eve knew the damage was done. They couldn't hide their sin from God. It was hard to face his disappointment. "I'm sorry you disobeyed me. It means you have to leave this beautiful garden."

The Lord God sent Adam and Eve from the garden.

Eve cried as they left the garden. "I'm so sorry. I didn't mean to disobey—the snake made it sound so good."

"I know, child, I know. I have to punish you for disobeying, but—I still love you. I always will."

"I can take the punishment," Eve cried, "if I know that you still love me. I love you, too. I always will."

Based on Genesis 3

Becoming a Woman of God

A Woman of God accepts the consequences for choices she makes

Eve was made in God's image, but she was free to make her own choices. She made a bad choice when she chose to disobey God. God punished Adam and Eve. They had to accept the consequences of the choices they made. That means Eve had to accept the punishment for her bad choice.

When have you made a bad choice? Were you punished for disobeying?

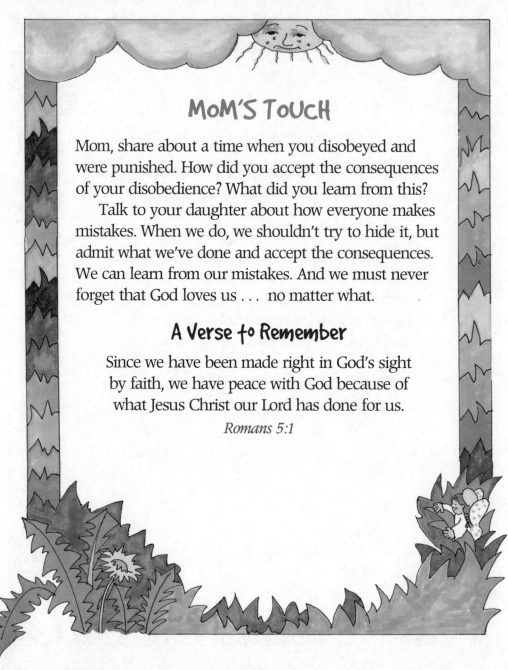

MoM'S TOUCH

Mom, share about a time when you disobeyed and were punished. How did you accept the consequences of your disobedience? What did you learn from this?

Talk to your daughter about how everyone makes mistakes. When we do, we shouldn't try to hide it, but admit what we've done and accept the consequences. We can learn from our mistakes. And we must never forget that God loves us ... no matter what.

A Verse to Remember

Since we have been made right in God's sight by faith, we have peace with God because of what Jesus Christ our Lord has done for us.

Romans 5:1

Whatever You Say, Dear

"You're going to build a what?" Mrs. Noah asked.

"An ark," Mr. Noah repeated. "A boat, my dear! A big, big boat!"

"A boat? A boat? Where do you get these crazy ideas?"

"From God," Noah replied quietly.

"Gulp. Did you say God?" Mrs. Noah nervously brushed the flour from her hands as Noah explained that God was tired of the way people were behaving. It wasn't a surprise really. People had become selfish and rotten. God had tried so many times to get them to listen to him. He must have finally given up.

"God has decided to wipe out every living thing," Noah explained. "Everything on earth will die in a big flood. Then God will begin the human race again—with us."

"But we don't have any children," Mrs. Noah objected.

"You'd better start knitting booties, my dear. I think God has a plan for us," Noah smiled.

"Well," said Mrs. Noah, "if God wants you to build an ark, you'd better get busy!"

By the time the ark was built, Mrs. Noah had three sons— and they were all grown up and married.

As Noah put on the finishing touches, there was a strange clomping sound. Mrs. Noah looked up and saw a parade of animals coming toward them. "NOAH! What's going on here?" she cried.

"Um, did I mention that God is sending a few animals to go in the ark?" Noah mumbled.

"With us? We're going in the boat with those wild, smelly animals?" Mrs. Noah wondered.

"We'd better. Flood coming, you know."

Mrs. Noah looked at the lions, bears, and spiders (did there have to be spiders?). She smiled and took Noah's hand. "Whatever you say, dear."

Based on Genesis 6:1–7:9

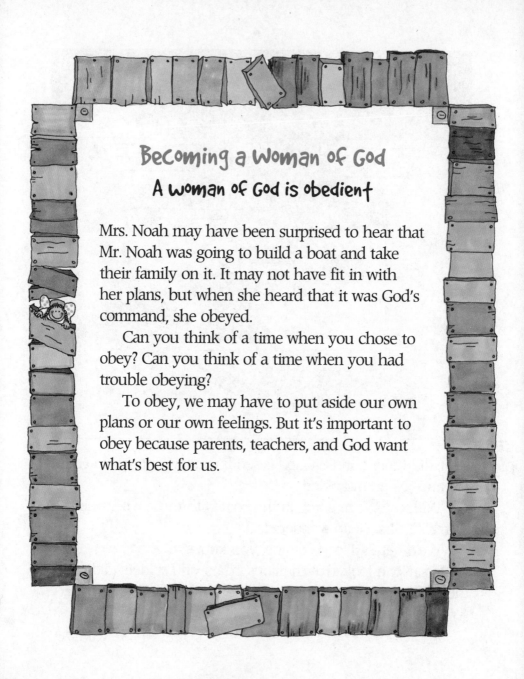

Becoming a Woman of God
A Woman of God is obedient

Mrs. Noah may have been surprised to hear that Mr. Noah was going to build a boat and take their family on it. It may not have fit in with her plans, but when she heard that it was God's command, she obeyed.

Can you think of a time when you chose to obey? Can you think of a time when you had trouble obeying?

To obey, we may have to put aside our own plans or our own feelings. But it's important to obey because parents, teachers, and God want what's best for us.

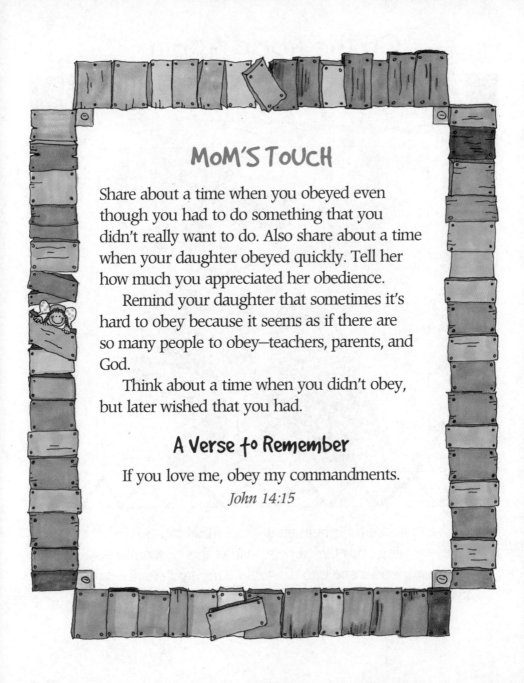

MoM'S TOUCH

Share about a time when you obeyed even though you had to do something that you didn't really want to do. Also share about a time when your daughter obeyed quickly. Tell her how much you appreciated her obedience.

Remind your daughter that sometimes it's hard to obey because it seems as if there are so many people to obey—teachers, parents, and God.

Think about a time when you didn't obey, but later wished that you had.

A Verse to Remember

If you love me, obey my commandments.

John 14:15

On the Road Again

Sarah packed their belongings and Abraham tied everything onto the camels. Just as she closed the last bag, her best friend came into the tent. "Sarah, you're not really leaving, are you? I'll miss you so much."

"It's hard for me too, but God said that we should go—so we go," Sarah said kindly. "God promised that if we obey him, he will give us as many descendants as there are the stars in the sky!" The couple had no children and Sarah's heart ached to be a mother.

We can trust God to keep his promises

Sarah held onto Abraham's
hand as they left Haran with
their servants, the servants'
families, and all their animals.
Their friends lined the road,
watching sadly. Even the little
children were sad to see the
kindly couple leave.

The caravan moved slowly, trusting God to lead them. "Miss Sarah, will you sing to me while we walk?"

"Of course, little one," Sarah smiled. Soon a large group of children surrounded Sarah, talking with her and listening to her songs about God's love and care.

Sarah often wished they could stop traveling and stay in one place for awhile. But she and Abraham were a team, and they tried to always obey God. Deep in Sarah's heart God's promise was still alive: Someday they would have children of their own.

Based on Genesis 12:1–9

Becoming a Woman of God

A Woman of God
trusts in God's promises

God promised Abraham and Sarah that someday they would have as many descendants as there were stars in the sky. But when they were very old, they still didn't have any children.

Sometimes we have to wait a long time for God's promises to be fulfilled. Waiting is very hard to do, but waiting teaches us to trust God.

When have you had to wait a long time for a promise to be kept? What was it?

Mom's Touch

Share a story about a time you trusted God and waited for something. Perhaps you were waiting for God's guidance to know what he wanted you to do.

Explain that sometimes we don't get what we pray for, but we're changed in the process.

Help your daughter understand that waiting on God is not easy. But it helps us learn to trust him. When we get impatient we can tell him how we feel and ask him to help us trust him more.

A Verse to Remember

Trust in the LORD with all your heart;
do not depend on your own understanding.

Proverbs 3:5

A Dangerous Giggle

Sarah listened from inside the tent as the three strangers promised her ninety-nine-year-old husband that she would have a baby by this time next year. *How long have we waited for God to keep his promise?* she thought. *Now he's going to keep it? Now? When I'm old and wrinkled?*

As Sarah smoothed down her dress she saw her wrinkled hands covered with bulging veins and age spots. Suddenly the very thought of her ancient body carrying a baby struck Sarah funny. Before she could stop it, a deep rumbling giggle started down in her belly and rolled up through her body until it spilled out her mouth.

The men sitting outside with Abraham suddenly stopped talking. "Why did Sarah laugh at our news?" they asked. "Is anything too hard for God?"

"Laugh, who laughed?" Sarah defended herself. Poor Abraham looked from the men to Sarah and back again. He was completely confused.

Several months later it was obvious that the men's message had been from God. "Abraham, I can barely see my feet anymore!" Sarah giggled. "Oh, come quick!" Abraham hurried to Sarah and laid his hand on her stomach. He felt the baby growing inside her wiggle and kick.

Nearly a year after the visit by the three men, Abraham and Sarah became parents of a baby boy. They named him "Isaac," which means laughter. Sarah cradled the small miracle in her arms and whispered, "Praise God for promises kept!"

Based on Genesis 18:1–15; 21:1–7

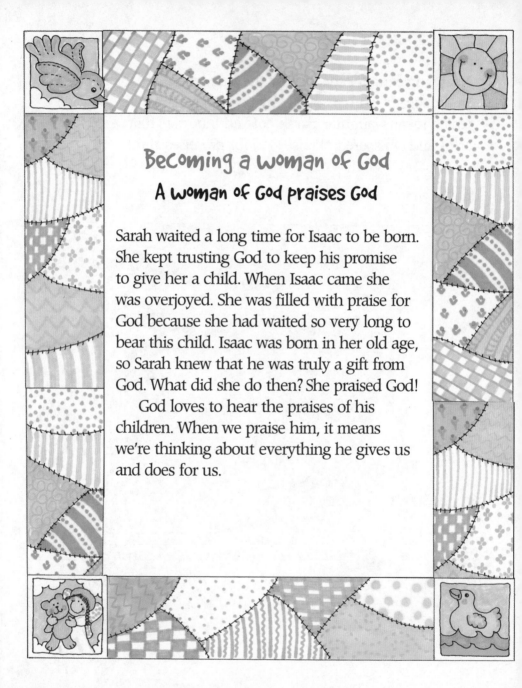

Becoming a Woman of God
A Woman of God Praises God

Sarah waited a long time for Isaac to be born. She kept trusting God to keep his promise to give her a child. When Isaac came she was overjoyed. She was filled with praise for God because she had waited so very long to bear this child. Isaac was born in her old age, so Sarah knew that he was truly a gift from God. What did she do then? She praised God!

God loves to hear the praises of his children. When we praise him, it means we're thinking about everything he gives us and does for us.

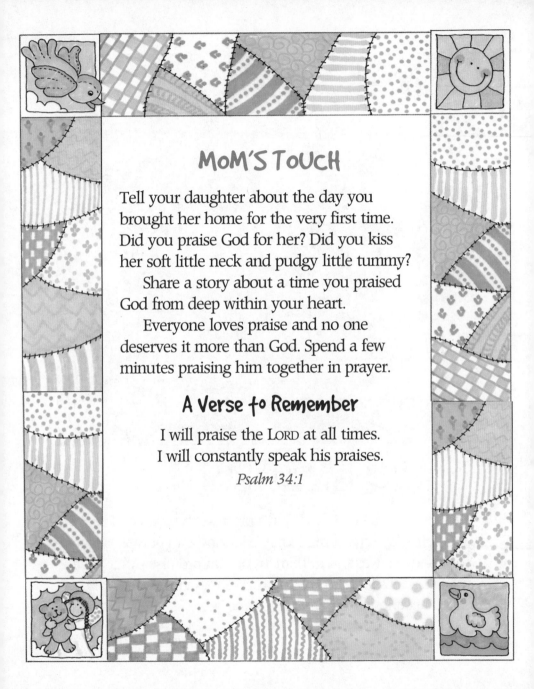

MoM'S TOUCH

Tell your daughter about the day you brought her home for the very first time. Did you praise God for her? Did you kiss her soft little neck and pudgy little tummy?

Share a story about a time you praised God from deep within your heart.

Everyone loves praise and no one deserves it more than God. Spend a few minutes praising him together in prayer.

A Verse to Remember

I will praise the LORD at all times.
I will constantly speak his praises.

Psalm 34:1

Eviction!

Abraham remembered God's promise that he would someday have a big family. He thought perhaps Hagar's son, Ishmael, was the fulfillment of that promise. After all, he was Ishmael's father. What neither Abraham nor Hagar knew was that serious trouble was coming.

Oddly enough, the problem was Sarah, Abraham's wife. She felt that her son, Isaac, was the answer to God's promise—not Ishmael. So when Sarah saw Ishmael teasing Isaac one day, she ran to Abraham and demanded, "Get rid of that woman and her son!"

Abraham sadly gave Hagar and Ishmael food and water and sent them away. In a few days when the food and water were gone, Hagar got scared. "How am I going to take care of my son? What's going to happen to us?" Just then Ishmael started to cry, "I want to go home."

Hagar's heart broke. She walked off a little way from her son and dropped to her knees, weeping. "I don't want to watch my boy die!"

When Hagar looked up, an angel was beside her, "Don't cry.
God heard your son's cries. Look, God made a well over there
so you can get your son a drink. God wants you to know that
Ishmael will be fine. In fact, one day he will be the leader of a
great nation."

Based on Genesis 21:8–21

Becoming a Woman of God

A Woman of God takes her problems to him

Hagar was very upset. She may have felt that she had no place to turn. Actually, the best place we can ever go for help is to God.

God loves his children very much and he cares about all the problems we have. No problem is too big or too small to take to God.

We can talk to him when someone we love is sick, when we're having problems with friends, or when we're lonely or sad.

Are there some things that you would like to talk to God about right now? What are they?

MoM'S TOUCH

This is a good chance to show your daughter that you have problems, too, and that you take your problems to God. Tell her about some time in the past when you had a problem. Tell her how you talked to God about it. If the situation has been solved, tell her how God helped you with the problem.

A mother's love and care are so strong that her children's problems are as painful to her as her own. Talk to your daughter about how you feel when she's having a problem. Tell her how much you care and that when she's sad, you're sad, too.

A Verse to Remember

Don't worry about anything;
instead, pray about everything.
Tell God what you need,
and thank him for all he has done.

Philippians 4:6

A Mother's Worst Nightmare

Sarah knew Abraham wasn't telling her the whole story. A wife can tell those things. When he told her that he was taking Isaac to the mountains to make a sacrifice to God, there was a catch in his throat. He just didn't sound like the Abraham she knew.

An alarm went off in Sarah's heart when Abraham and Isaac left with the wood and fire for the sacrifice—but no lamb. Sarah heard Isaac ask, "Where is the lamb?"

"God will provide, my son," Abraham answered. Sarah's heart twisted with fear as she watched them leave. Then she went inside and prayed.

The days dragged by slowly until the afternoon Sarah heard Isaac's sweet voice calling her. "Mother, wait until you hear what God did!" The story of how God took care of Sarah's precious son and blessed her wonderful husband spilled out from Isaac.

"Father tied me up and put me on the altar. I was going to be the sacrifice." Sarah's jaw dropped open as she looked at Abraham. He smiled understandingly and raised his finger to his lips before she could speak.

"Just when Father was about to . . . well, an angel of God said, 'Stop! Now I know that you fear God more than anything.' Then we saw a ram stuck in a bush. So, Father and I sacrificed it to God."

Sarah grabbed Isaac and held him tightly, more grateful than ever for God's constant love.

Based on Genesis 22:1–14

Becoming a Woman of God
A Woman of God loves God most of all

Sarah isn't the person in this story whom we usually think of as the one being tested. But she certainly learned a powerful lesson—nothing and no one should be more important than God.

Is there anything in your life that is sometimes more important to you than God? It might be a thing or a person, or maybe it's the town where you live—you wouldn't be willing to move to a new place, even if God wanted you to.

MOM'S TOUCH

Tell your daughter how very much you love her and that you thank God every day for the privilege of being her mother.

Share about a time when you struggled with something becoming more important than God. What was crowding God out? How did you handle it?

Talk about what is important to your daughter and discuss how to keep things in proper perspective.

A Verse to Remember

You must love the LORD your God
with all your heart, all your soul,
and all your strength.

Deuteronomy 6:5

Of course Rebekah loved Esau. After all, he was her firstborn son. But Jacob was . . . special. He often helped around the house, and as they worked they talked about Jacob's dreams. So, when Rebekah heard Isaac say that he was ready to pass on the family blessing to Esau, an honor given to the oldest son of the family, a plan began to take shape in her mind.

"I want you to get that blessing!" Rebekah told Jacob. "Whoever gets that blessing will lead the family. It must be you! Your father asked Esau to make his favorite meal before he gives the blessing. Bring me two goats and I'll cook a meal. You will take it to your father before Esau returns and you will get the blessing."

"But I . . ."

"Be quiet. Just do what I tell you to do!"

After Rebekah cooked, she helped Jacob put goatskins on his arms so his skin would feel hairy like Esau's. He put on Esau's clothes and took the food to his father. Rebekah hid outside and listened. Old Isaac was blind and easily confused. "You sound like Jacob, but you feel and smell like Esau," he said.

"I am Esau, Father. Give me the blessing!" Jacob insisted.

Convinced this must be his oldest son, Isaac said, "My beloved Esau, may God bless you richly, may nations serve you, and may you rule over your brothers."

Barely able to control his joy, Jacob ran out and hugged his mother. Together they danced and celebrated.

When Esau came back, he begged Isaac for the blessing, but it was too late—once it was given, it couldn't be changed! Esau angrily vowed to get even with his brother. *Jacob must leave*, Rebekah thought. With her heart breaking, Rebekah watched her son go. "What have I done?" she cried. "Jacob has the blessing—that's what I wanted, but I may never see him again."

Based on Genesis 27:1–28:6

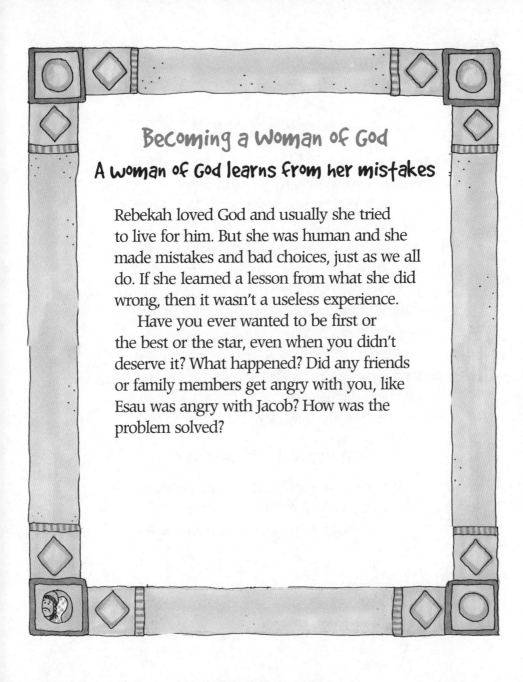

Becoming a Woman of God
A woman of God learns from her mistakes

Rebekah loved God and usually she tried to live for him. But she was human and she made mistakes and bad choices, just as we all do. If she learned a lesson from what she did wrong, then it wasn't a useless experience.

Have you ever wanted to be first or the best or the star, even when you didn't deserve it? What happened? Did any friends or family members get angry with you, like Esau was angry with Jacob? How was the problem solved?

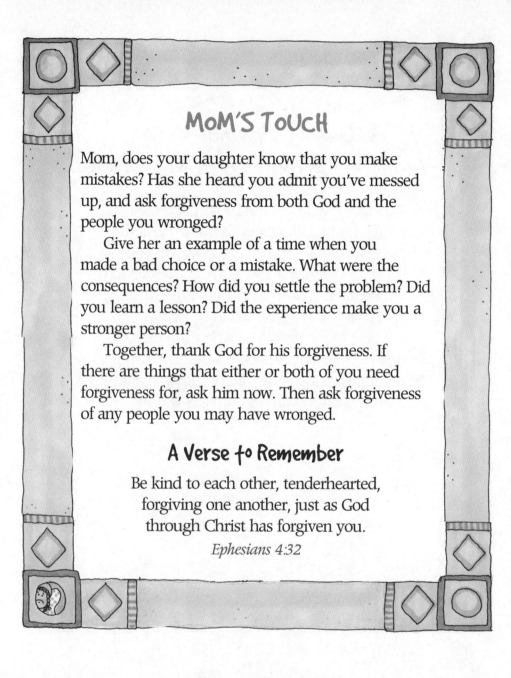

MOM'S TOUCH

Mom, does your daughter know that you make mistakes? Has she heard you admit you've messed up, and ask forgiveness from both God and the people you wronged?

Give her an example of a time when you made a bad choice or a mistake. What were the consequences? How did you settle the problem? Did you learn a lesson? Did the experience make you a stronger person?

Together, thank God for his forgiveness. If there are things that either or both of you need forgiveness for, ask him now. Then ask forgiveness of any people you may have wronged.

A Verse to Remember

Be kind to each other, tenderhearted,
forgiving one another, just as God
through Christ has forgiven you.

Ephesians 4:32

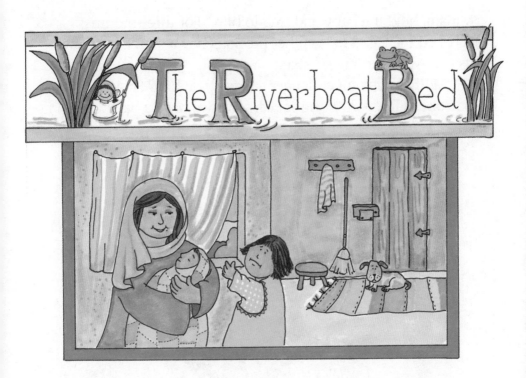

The Riverboat Bed

"I don't care what Pharaoh ordered. I can't give him up. Just look at him, he's beautiful. I know God has wonderful plans for my son!" Jochebed hugged her newborn baby, promising herself to protect him from Pharaoh's soldiers—even though they had orders to kill all Hebrew baby boys.

"Miriam, hold the baby and sing to him." For three months Jochebed managed to keep her precious boy a secret, but now his cries were getting stronger.

"Mother, how much longer can we hide him? Sooner or later someone will report to the soldiers that we have a baby here."

"I won't let my son die. Go to the river and pick some reeds for me. I have a plan." Jochebed worked quickly, humming to herself as she wove reeds into a small basket, then covered it with tar. Miriam held the baby and watched her mother work, wondering what on earth she was doing.

Then Jochebed held her son close, feeling his soft skin and enjoying his baby smell. Then she laid him in the basket, knowing she might never see him again. She carried the basket to the river and set it afloat. "Miriam, stay here and keep watch," Jochebed whispered as tears crawled down her cheeks. "Please God, take care of my baby," she prayed as she slowly walked home.

Jochebed's arms ached for her son as she waited for Miriam's report. Finally, Miriam burst into the room. "Pharaoh's daughter found the baby. She's going to keep him but she needs a nurse for him. Come quick! You can be his nurse!"

"Praise God," Jochebed prayed, "for taking care of my son!"

Based on Exodus 2:1–10

Becoming a Woman of God
A Woman of God is active

More than anything, Jochebed wanted her son to live. She believed that he should live. So, she did something about it. She did what she could and God did the rest. He took care of Moses.

There are times to wait and times to work. When you believe that something needs to be done, ask God for his help and wisdom, and then get moving!

When have you gotten involved in working on something that needed to be done? When have you not done something and later wished that you had gotten involved?

MoM'S TOUCH

When was a time you knew God was leading you to do something? Talk about how to be busy and still be open to God's leading. Talk about the ways we know God is leading us: through his Word, through our prayers, through people we respect, through our strong feelings, through opportunities we have.

Ask your daughter if she thinks God is asking her to take action about something. Ask her why she thinks this. Then pray together for the courage to act when and how God would want you to.

A Verse to Remember

Lead me by your truth and teach me,
for you are the God who saves me.
All day long I put my hope in you.

Psalm 25:5

My Brother's Keeper

Miriam wiggled through the crowd. She wanted to hear everything that was being said. The angry people were shouting at her brother, "Why did you come here? Since you asked Pharaoh to let us leave Egypt, he's just made us work harder! Go away! Leave us alone!" Miriam sighed. She still had the urge to take care of her baby brother.

Miriam's heart ached for Moses. He was only doing what God told him to do and yet the people were so angry. "Trust God," Moses told them. "He wants to free you from slavery!" But the people wouldn't listen.

God is going to have to do something big to convince these people, Miriam thought.

Miriam knew that God had done something big when all the water in Egypt turned to blood. Even the Nile River!

"What will we drink? The fish are dead! Ick! It smells!" The Egyptians panicked.

Moses and God did it, Miriam thought. *Now the Egyptians will know that God is boss!*

But Pharaoh refused to let the Israelites leave.

Moses has to come up with something more convincing than this, thought Miriam. Sure enough, each time Moses asked and each time Pharaoh refused to let the people leave, something awful happened to the Egyptians. Frogs filled the land or gnats bugged the Egyptians, then hail killed their crops. On and on it went until nine terrible things happened to the Egyptians.

But Pharaoh was stubborn. He refused to let the Israelites leave. Miriam was amazed at her brother's total trust in God. She wondered what God and Moses would do next to get Pharaoh's attention. *At least he has the Israelites' attention. No one is criticizing Moses anymore,* she thought. Everyone, including Miriam, waited to see what God would do next.

Based on Exodus 7:1–10:29

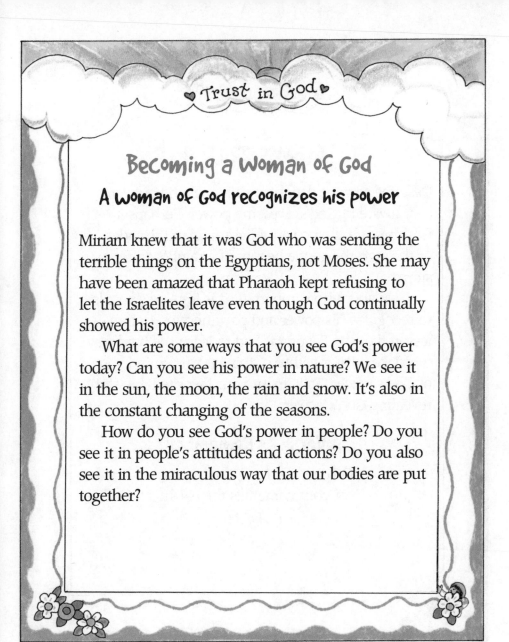

Becoming a Woman of God
A Woman of God recognizes his power

Miriam knew that it was God who was sending the terrible things on the Egyptians, not Moses. She may have been amazed that Pharaoh kept refusing to let the Israelites leave even though God continually showed his power.

What are some ways that you see God's power today? Can you see his power in nature? We see it in the sun, the moon, the rain and snow. It's also in the constant changing of the seasons.

How do you see God's power in people? Do you see it in people's attitudes and actions? Do you also see it in the miraculous way that our bodies are put together?

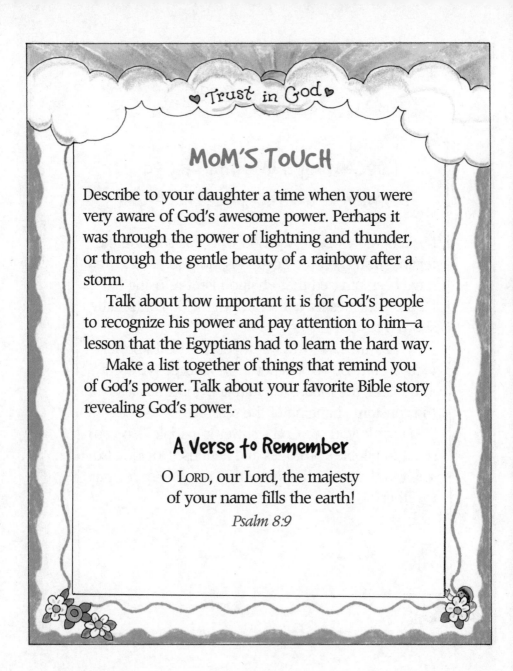

MOM'S TOUCH

Describe to your daughter a time when you were very aware of God's awesome power. Perhaps it was through the power of lightning and thunder, or through the gentle beauty of a rainbow after a storm.

Talk about how important it is for God's people to recognize his power and pay attention to him—a lesson that the Egyptians had to learn the hard way.

Make a list together of things that remind you of God's power. Talk about your favorite Bible story revealing God's power.

A Verse to Remember

O LORD, our Lord, the majesty
of your name fills the earth!

Psalm 8:9

Saving the Worst for Last

Miriam hugged her oldest child as she watched her husband paint the doorframe of their house with lamb's blood. "Moses says this will keep us safe from the last plague. It's going to be a terrible one! The firstborn son in every Egyptian home will die tonight." A lump rose in Miriam's throat at the very thought. Oh, why hadn't Pharaoh just listened to Moses?

That night
hundreds of Egyptian
children died—even Pharaoh's
son. Through his tears, Pharaoh
told Moses, "Get out of Egypt."

Miriam's heart ached for the poor
Egyptian mothers, as she hugged her
children. A huge cloud led the Israelites out
of Egypt. God was in the cloud, so the Israelites
always knew he was leading them.

Finally, Moses said they should set up camp near the Red Sea.
Miriam gratefully rubbed her tired feet. She longed to talk to her
brother, but he was so busy. Later, Miriam was making dinner
when she heard shouting. Panic gripped her heart when she saw a
cloud of dust in the distance. Pharaoh had changed his mind about
their freedom. His army was chasing them!

Now what will the people do? Miriam wondered. She wasn't
surprised when they got angry with Moses. "Did you bring us out
here to die? Weren't there enough graves in Egypt?" How would
Moses answer?

"Watch what God will do for you!" Moses shouted. Miriam held her breath as her brother climbed onto a rock and held his staff over the Red Sea. Suddenly, the waters rolled and parted into two big water walls.

All the Israelites walked through the sea on dry ground. Miriam remembered watching Moses' basketboat on the Nile River many years before. *Mother was right,* she thought. *God did have great plans for Moses.* The last Israelite came through the sea and the Egyptians raced in, but the water crashed down on them. Every soldier died. Miriam grabbed a tambourine and sang with joy, "Praise the LORD for a wonderful victory!"

Based on Exodus 11:1–15:21

Becoming a Woman of God
A woman of God looks for God's bigger plan

Miriam saw all ten of the plagues that were put on Egypt. She understood that God would stop sending plagues anytime that Pharaoh let the Israelites leave. Then when the Egyptians seemed to have the Israelites trapped, she saw God rescue them again. As Miriam looked back over all that had happened, she could surely see God's hand in each circumstance.

Seeing God's plan unfold helps our trust and confidence in him to grow. How does this story make you feel about trusting God?

MoM'S TOUCH

Share a time when something happened to you that was upsetting or even dangerous. When you stepped back from the situation, could you see that it was part of God's bigger plan?

Explain to your daughter how a piece of stitchery may look pretty from the front, but when you look at the back you see how many complicated stitches it took to make the lovely piece. God's big plan is somewhat like that. One stitch is not beautiful by itself, but all the stitches together create a beautiful tapestry.

A Verse to Remember

Shout with joy to the LORD, O earth!
Worship the LORD with gladness.
Come before him, singing with joy.

Psalm 100:1–2

Eating Out!

It seemed like everywhere the Hebrew woman went, people were complaining. "Why did Moses drag us out to this desert? At least in Egypt we had food to eat," she sighed. "I'm hungry, too. And it's hard to hear my children cry that they're hungry when I have nothing to give them."

Mostly out of curiosity, the woman went along when the people went to Moses and demanded to know what he was going to do about their problems. She was surprised to hear Moses announce, "God has heard your cries. Every morning he will give you food from heaven, and every evening he will send you meat." *I want to believe Moses,* the troubled woman thought, *but does he know what he's talking about?*

Later that day, the woman's stomach was growling when she heard an odd noise. Peeking out of her tent, she saw hundreds, maybe thousands of birds on the ground. People grabbed them and rushed to cook and eat them. *Wow*, she thought, *this is just like Moses said. Now, I wonder what the other part of Moses' report meant.*

For the first night in a very long time, the woman and her children went to bed with full tummies. It felt so good to be satisfied that the tired mother fell asleep instantly, not even thinking about the rest of God's promise. So the next morning, she was as puzzled as everyone else about the white flakes covering the ground.

"What is it?" the woman asked.

"Manna," someone answered. "It's God's gift of food to us. Taste it, it's sweet. It will make good bread."

She thoughtfully bit into the crunchy white wafer. *God's gift of food . . . food from heaven. So this is what Moses meant. Thank you, God, for taking care of us!*

Based on Exodus 16

Becoming a Woman of God

A woman of God knows God meets her daily needs

The woman in this story learned that God cared about her smallest needs. She, and the other Israelites, were simply hungry. God cared about their need. He helped them.

Have you thought about how God takes care of you every day? Think about all the things you do from the time you wake up each morning until you go to bed at night. Have you thanked God lately for his daily care?

MOM'S TOUCH

Have you ever been very hungry or thirsty? Has there ever been a time when you needed God to meet your basic needs of food, clothing, or shelter? Tell your daughter how God took care of you.

Perhaps you've been blessed with always having your needs met, but have volunteered in shelters or homes where people are not so fortunate. Tell your daughter how you felt in that situation.

Make a list together of all that God does for you in a single day. Post it on the refrigerator and thank him every day for his loving care.

A Verse to Remember

It is good to give thanks to the LORD,
to sing praises to the Most High.

Psalm 92:1

THE PERFECT TEN

I'm tired, Zipporah thought. Since leaving Egypt the Israelites had walked for three straight months. Now they were camped at the foot of Mt. Sinai, and she just wanted to rest. Of course, when your husband is in charge of leading more than 2 million Israelites, there really isn't much chance for rest.

Moses came in just as Zipporah was lying down for a short nap. "I'm going up on the mountain," he told her.

"Now? We just got settled. Can't you rest for a while? You must be tired."

"I am tired, but God called me so I must go," Moses said.

When Moses came back, he announced that God wanted to speak to all the people. Three days later, Zipporah's heart was pounding as she stood with the other Israelites at the base of Mt. Sinai. Thunder and lightning crashed on the mountain and a thick dark cloud covered it. Zipporah could hardly catch her breath.

I wonder if this is the way God always speaks to my husband, she thought. (It was more than a little bit frightening!) Zipporah was more impressed than ever with Moses' courage and his position before God. People around her shook and trembled in fear as Moses disappeared into the cloud to speak with God alone.

Worship God only.

Do not make idols to worship.

Be careful how to use God's name.

Rest on God's day.

Honor your father and mother.

Do not murder.

Keep your marriage pure.

Do not steal.

Do not lie.

Do not want things that belong to others.

Days later Zipporah prayed, "God, I know you are protecting Moses, but he has been gone a long time." Zipporah admitted to herself that she would feel better when her husband was home.

When he did return, Zipporah was surprised to see that Moses was holding two slabs of stone. "They're rules," he told her. "God himself wrote ten rules for the people to live by."

Based on Exodus 18:5; 19:1–20:21

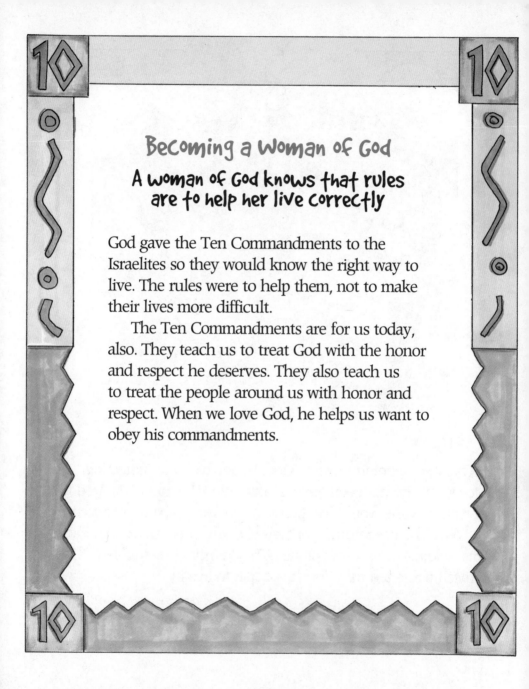

Becoming a Woman of God

A Woman of God knows that rules are to help her live correctly

God gave the Ten Commandments to the Israelites so they would know the right way to live. The rules were to help them, not to make their lives more difficult.

The Ten Commandments are for us today, also. They teach us to treat God with the honor and respect he deserves. They also teach us to treat the people around us with honor and respect. When we love God, he helps us want to obey his commandments.

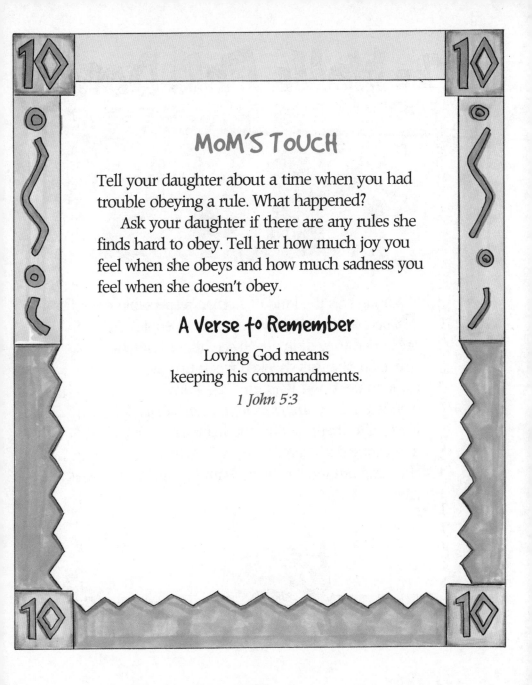

MoM'S Touch

Tell your daughter about a time when you had trouble obeying a rule. What happened?

Ask your daughter if there are any rules she finds hard to obey. Tell her how much joy you feel when she obeys and how much sadness you feel when she doesn't obey.

A Verse to Remember

Loving God means
keeping his commandments.

1 John 5:3

The Walls Fall Down!

Rahab was the kind of woman respectable people stayed away from. Most people pretended they didn't even see her on the street. So, she was shocked when two men came to her door. *Who are these guys?* she wondered. *They aren't from Jericho.* Rahab listened to them talking and made an interesting discovery. "They're Israelites checking out Jericho. They want to capture our city."

Actually, Rahab had a strong respect for the Israelites. She knew how powerful their God was. So, when soldiers came looking for the spies, she made a quick decision. "Hide on the roof. I'll get rid of the soldiers," she told the two men.

She came back to the spies and said, "I risked my life to save you; will you protect me when you capture the city?" The spies agreed and gave her a red rope to hang in her window so they would be able to find her quickly.

The Israelite army arrived a few weeks later. Rahab packed her things and waited to be rescued. But for six days the Israelites just silently marched around the city—once a day. *What are they doing? Why don't they just attack?* Rahab wondered, getting more nervous each day. The Israelites kept on marching.

On the seventh day the Israelites began their daily march. But they didn't stop after marching once around the city. They marched around and around. *This must be the day*, Rahab thought. She didn't even realize she was so nervous that she was holding her breath. Suddenly, the priests blew their horns and the Israelites shouted! Rahab screamed! The huge walls around Jericho began to crumble and fall.

...and the walls came a tumbling down...

JERICHO

Dust and screams filled the air as Rahab fell to her knees and prayed, "O Israelite God, please let the spies remember their promise." Just then a soldier grabbed her arm.

"Are you Rahab?" he shouted. She nodded and he said, "Come on, you've got to get out of here."

They remembered! "Thank you, God," Rahab prayed. "You are an awesome God."

Based on Joshua 6

Becoming a Woman of God

A Woman of God Chooses God even when those around her do not

When the spies first came to Jericho, Rahab might not have believed in God. But she had heard of the awesome things God had done to protect his people. She respected his power and chose to let his power protect her instead of destroy her. The other people in Jericho had surely heard the same stories, but they had chosen to ignore them and we know what happened to them!

Do you ever feel like the only one in your group of friends who cares anything at all about God? How can you gently show others by your life that God is important to you?

MOM'S TOUCH

Almost every Christian has met someone who makes fun of their faith or gives them a hard time about it. Share a time when you chose God even though those around you didn't. How did you feel? Were you scared? Lonely?

Assure your daughter that it's OK to not always go along with the crowd, especially if that means denying her faith in God.

Pray together that God will give you both the courage to live for God each day.

A Verse to Remember

What does the LORD your God require of you? He requires you to fear him, to live according to his will, to love and worship him with all your heart and soul.

Deuteronomy 10:12

How many times will God have to rescue my people from their foolishness? Deborah wondered. The Israelites had often turned away from God and then begged for his help when they were in trouble. Jabin's army had been beating up on them for twenty years now. And here were the Israelites . . . begging God to help them . . . again.

Deborah was a prophetess. She gave God's word to the people. It was a big job, especially because the people hardly ever listened to God's words. Many people brought their problems to her and she patiently told them what they should do. Then one day God told Deborah his plan for freeing the Israelites from Jabin.

Deborah immediately told Barak, "God says to take your army to Mt. Tabor. God will bring Sisera, Jabin's army commander, there. You can capture him!" Deborah bubbled with excitement.

But, Barak's response shocked her: "I will only go if you go with me!"

"What?" Deborah shouted. "If I come, a woman will get the credit for this victory, not you!"

Barak didn't care. He wanted Deborah with him.

It was a frustrated Deborah who marched up Mt. Tabor with Barak and his ten thousand men. Deborah and Barak saw the cloud of dust as Sisera and his nine hundred iron chariots approached. Deborah eagerly waited for Barak to command his army to attack, but he didn't. "Go on," she finally shouted. "God brought Sisera to you. Capture him!"

Deborah's words pushed Barak into action and the battle began.
But Sisera deserted his army and ran off to save his own life. Just as
Deborah had predicted, the honor of defeating Sisera and freeing the
Israelite people went to a woman. A woman named Jael killed Sisera
while he was sleeping. Deborah celebrated the victory with a song of
praise to God!

Based on Judges 4–5

Becoming a Woman of God
A woman of God can be a leader

Deborah had an important position in Israel. A prophetess served God by leading the people and fighting against their enemies. She must have been a very strong woman.

Deborah's job probably wasn't easy, but she knew it was important for the Israelites to defeat their enemies, so she did what she needed to do to make that happen.

Do you like leading, or would you rather be back in the crowd? Have you ever been the leader in getting your group of friends to do something? What was it?

MOM'S TOUCH

Tell your daughter about your elementary school days and the group of friends you had. Was there one person in the group who usually decided what the group would play or do? What different choices would you make now?

Discuss with your daughter what kinds of things it would be OK to go along with the crowd on . . . and what kinds of things she should say "no way" to.

A Verse to Remember

So be careful how you live,
not as fools but as those who are wise.

Ephesians 5:15

Ruth's husband was from another country. He didn't know her ways and she didn't really know his. All Ruth knew was that she loved him. He was a nice man whose family had moved to Moab because there was no food in their land. His widowed mother, Naomi, was sweet to Ruth and her sister-in-law, Orpah.

A FOREIGNER IN A FOREIGN LAND

Ruth had never dared to dream she could be so happy. It was almost too good to be true. But one dark day everything changed. Ruth's and Orpah's husbands died. Both of them. Ruth's heart ached so much that she thought it would break. Ruth, Orpah and Naomi cried together for their dead husbands.

Ruth didn't think things
could get any worse, until Naomi decided to return to Judah. "I
won't let you go alone," Ruth declared. Orpah came along, too.

But soon after they began the trip, Naomi said, "Go home, girls.
You're young, you can marry again. Go home to your people." Orpah
did go back home. But Ruth promised to stay with Naomi.

Once Ruth and Naomi got to Judah, they had no jobs and no money. They often didn't know where their next meal was coming from. Then Ruth took charge. She went to a grain field that belonged to a man named Boaz. Ruth picked up any grain left on the ground by the workers.

OBED

"Boaz is a nice man who treats his workers kindly," Ruth reported to Naomi.

"Ruth works hard and is very loyal to Naomi," Boaz's friends told him. Soon Boaz and Ruth married and had a baby boy. Their son would be an ancestor of Jesus Christ.

Based on the Book of Ruth

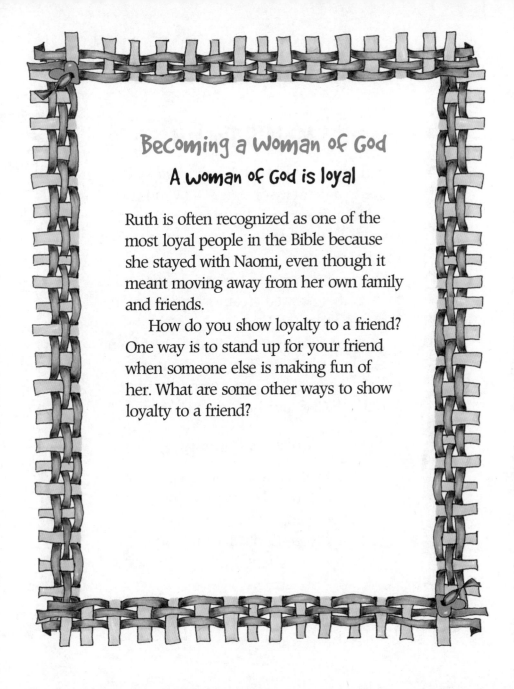

Becoming a Woman of God
A woman of God is loyal

Ruth is often recognized as one of the most loyal people in the Bible because she stayed with Naomi, even though it meant moving away from her own family and friends.

How do you show loyalty to a friend? One way is to stand up for your friend when someone else is making fun of her. What are some other ways to show loyalty to a friend?

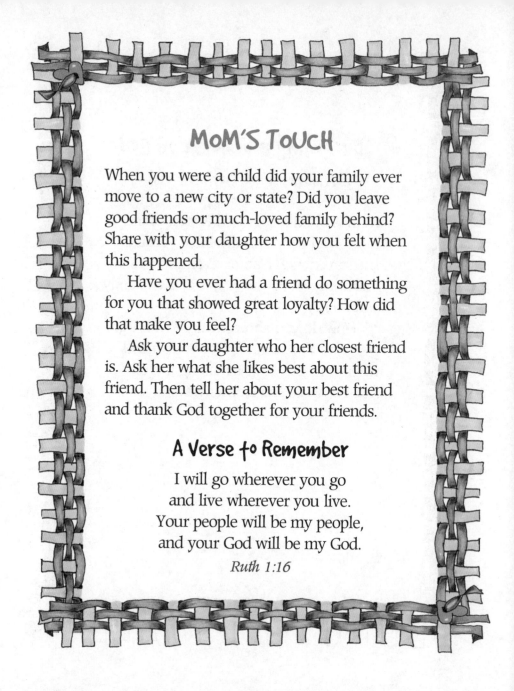

MOM'S TOUCH

When you were a child did your family ever move to a new city or state? Did you leave good friends or much-loved family behind? Share with your daughter how you felt when this happened.

Have you ever had a friend do something for you that showed great loyalty? How did that make you feel?

Ask your daughter who her closest friend is. Ask her what she likes best about this friend. Then tell her about your best friend and thank God together for your friends.

A Verse to Remember

I will go wherever you go
and live wherever you live.
Your people will be my people,
and your God will be my God.

Ruth 1:16

The Shame of Shames

"Useless! That's what you are. What good is a wife who can't give her husband a child!" Peninnah constantly insulted Hannah. They had the same husband but the two women definitely did not like each other. Peninnah seldom missed an opportunity to brag that she had several children but Hannah did not have even one child.

"Hannah, I love you. It doesn't matter to me that you have no children." Elkanah often tried to comfort her. But the cry deep in Hannah's heart could not be silenced. Of course, Peninnah made sure that Hannah was constantly reminded of her failure to have a child.

One year, Elkanah and Hannah went to Shiloh to worship God at the temple. Hannah's heart was filled with sadness as she knelt at the altar. "Please, God," she sobbed. "Please see how very miserable I am. God, I promise that if you will bless me with a child, I will give him back to you, to serve you."

Eli, the priest, was watching Hannah at the altar. Her lips were moving but he could hear no sound. Eli didn't know the pain in Hannah's heart or the honesty of her prayer. "What do you mean by coming to God's temple when you are so drunk that you don't make sense?" he scolded her.

"I haven't been drinking. I have been pouring out my heart, begging God to give me a baby," Hannah told Eli.

Some time later Hannah did have a baby—a son whom she named Samuel—which means "Because I asked the Lord for him." Hannah remembered her promise to God; so when Samuel was old enough, she took him to live with Eli at the temple. Samuel helped Eli and learned to serve God. Hannah came to visit Samuel once a year and brought him a new robe.

Based on 1 Samuel 1

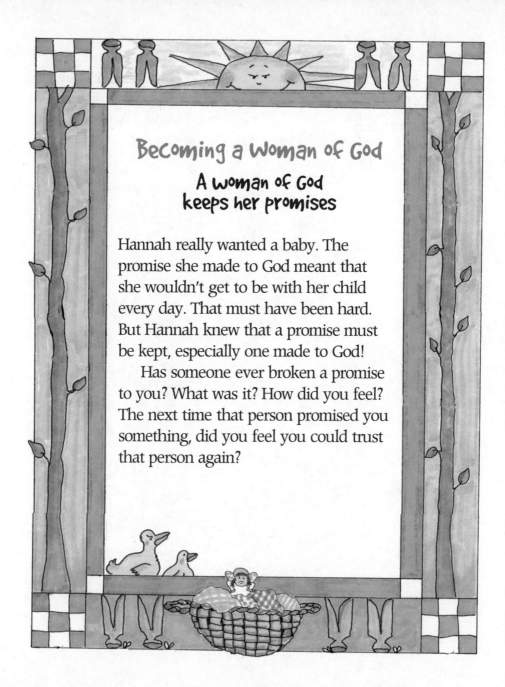

Becoming a Woman of God

A Woman of God keeps her promises

Hannah really wanted a baby. The promise she made to God meant that she wouldn't get to be with her child every day. That must have been hard. But Hannah knew that a promise must be kept, especially one made to God!

Has someone ever broken a promise to you? What was it? How did you feel? The next time that person promised you something, did you feel you could trust that person again?

MOM'S TOUCH

Do you love being a mom? Tell your daughter how you felt when you found out you were going to be a mother. Do you understand how much Hannah wanted to have a child?

Talk to your daughter about how important it is to keep promises. Give her some examples from your life of promises kept or promises broken and what the results were.

Discuss with your daughter what kind of promises people make to God. Why is it important to keep promises made to God?

A Verse to Remember

The Lord hates those who don't keep their word, but he delights in those who do.

Proverbs 12:22

"Stubborn fool . . . he is so rude . . . makes people so angry. I'm tired of covering up his stupidity!" Abigail tossed food into baskets as quickly as her hands would move, all the time complaining about her husband, Nabal. She was right. Nabal was rude and mean. And this time, Nabal had gone too far.

"I don't know if I can help him out this time. He has made David angry. King David!!!! Everyone knows about David—I mean we sing songs about his victories. He's our hero!

"All David wanted was a little food. It wouldn't have been hard for Nabal to give him food for his soldiers. After all, while they camped by us last year, we didn't have a single problem."

"But no—Nabal makes a nasty comment about why should he give his food to a lousy band of outlaws. Oh my, David is going to kill him. He's just going to kill him."

Abigail finished packing bread, wine, meat, grains, raisin cakes, and fig cakes. She carried the baskets outside and tied them on donkeys. Then she climbed on a donkey and headed down the dusty road toward David's camp.

"I wish this donkey would walk faster," Abigail sighed. But a few minutes later, she looked up and saw David and his men coming up the hill–on their way to kill her husband.

When David got closer, Abigail called out, "Sir, my husband is a fool. I accept responsibility for what Nabal did. I didn't know about your request until it was too late, so I've brought you some food now."

"Sir, you've never done anything wrong in your whole life. Don't start now. Don't murder my husband; please forgive him," Abigail begged.

Abigail breathed a sigh of relief when David thanked her for stopping him from doing something wrong. She went home praising God that David had heard her pleas!

Based on 1 Samuel 25:1–35

Becoming a Woman of God
A Woman of God is a peacemaker

Abigail knew that her husband was in trouble. She came up with a plan and went out of her way to make peace with King David.

How do you feel when you are around people who are fighting or arguing? It's not much fun, is it? Have you ever tried to be a peacemaker and get your friends or family members to make up?

Has a friend tried to be a peacemaker for you? What do you think of Abigail's plan of taking gifts to give David in order to make peace?

Mom's Touch

When have you been a peacemaker? Have you ever been a peacemaker between your children? Can you give an example to your daughter? Ask her if she has ever been a peacemaker.

Discuss with your daughter some of the words a peacemaker can use, such as, "When you say that it makes me feel, . . ." "I really like it when you do . . . but, when you do . . . I feel bad."

A Verse to Remember

How wonderful it is, how pleasant,
when brothers live together in harmony!

Psalm 133:1

King Solomon's incredible wisdom was known around the world. It was a gift from God which the king used to help his people. That's why the sad mother went to Solomon with her problem. Her heart was filled with panic, and the woman truly believed that the king was her last hope.

The woman bowed before King Solomon. A second woman entered, holding a small baby in her arms. The first woman pointed to her and said, "We both had little babies. During the night her baby died, so she took my live baby and laid her dead baby beside me. This morning I was very upset when I thought my child had died."

"NO!" screamed the other woman. "She's lying. This live baby is mine and the dead one is hers!"

Solomon looked at both women as he thought about what to do. Suddenly he ordered his servant, "Bring a sword. Cut this child in two and give half to each woman!" For a brief moment time seemed to stop. Neither woman dared to breathe.

"No!" the first woman screamed. "Don't hurt him. Let her have him." She fell on the floor, unable to stop crying.

At the same time the second woman held out the baby. "Fine!" she shouted. "Kill him! If I can't have him, then neither can she!"

King Solomon seemed to smile, as if he knew a secret. "Stop. Give the child to the first woman. She is his mother," he said.

The sobbing woman looked up. "H-H-How did you know?" she whispered.

Now King Solomon did smile. "Because the real mother would rather give up her child than let him be hurt." The woman hugged her child, knowing deep in her heart that the king's wisdom was truly a gift from God.

Based on 1 Kings 3:16–28

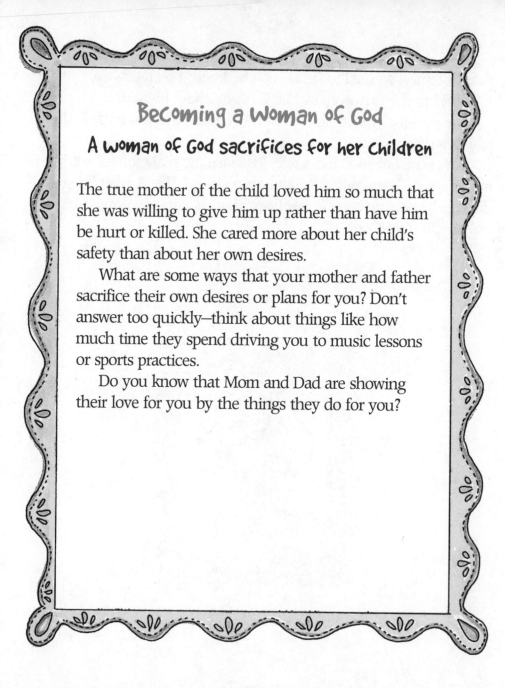

Becoming a Woman of God
A Woman of God sacrifices for her children

The true mother of the child loved him so much that she was willing to give him up rather than have him be hurt or killed. She cared more about her child's safety than about her own desires.

What are some ways that your mother and father sacrifice their own desires or plans for you? Don't answer too quickly—think about things like how much time they spend driving you to music lessons or sports practices.

Do you know that Mom and Dad are showing their love for you by the things they do for you?

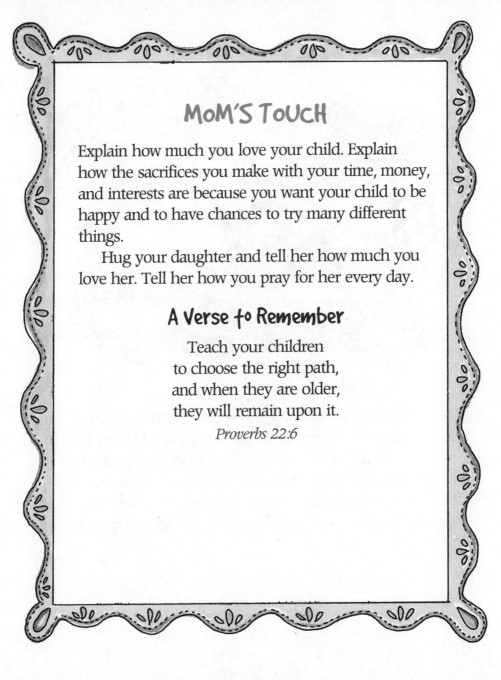

MOM'S TOUCH

Explain how much you love your child. Explain how the sacrifices you make with your time, money, and interests are because you want your child to be happy and to have chances to try many different things.

Hug your daughter and tell her how much you love her. Tell her how you pray for her every day.

A Verse to Remember

Teach your children
to choose the right path,
and when they are older,
they will remain upon it.

Proverbs 22:6

I'm so tired. If I could just sit down, the woman thought. For days she had skipped meals so her son would have food to eat. The woman's thoughts wandered to memories of when her husband was alive. Back then their dinner table was full— bread, meat, vegetables, and sweet cakes for dessert. She could almost smell the food, until her thoughts were interrupted.

A man's voice surprised her. "Excuse me, could I possibly have a drink of water?" She looked up to see Elijah, a prophet of God, standing there. The woman laid down the sticks she had been gathering and reached to get him a cup of water. "I could use a bite of bread, too," Elijah added. She choked back tears, knowing that she couldn't help him.

The woman looked over at her precious son. Her heart was filled with love for him, but fear of the future. "I wish I could help you," she whispered to Elijah. "But there isn't a bite of bread left in my house. I was just gathering sticks to cook up the little bit of flour and oil I have into a small loaf of bread. When that's gone, my son and I will starve to death."

The woman thought she was hearing things when Elijah said, "Don't worry about this. Go ahead and bake your loaf of bread. But make a small one for me first. You'll have plenty of flour and oil." The woman didn't have the strength to argue.

Surprisingly, after she had baked a small loaf for Elijah flour and oil were still left in her jars. She made food for herself and her son and again flour and oil were left over. The woman slowly regained her strength, all the time praising God because her flour and oil never ran out. "God is good. He has taken care of me and my son!"

Based on 1 Kings 17:8–16

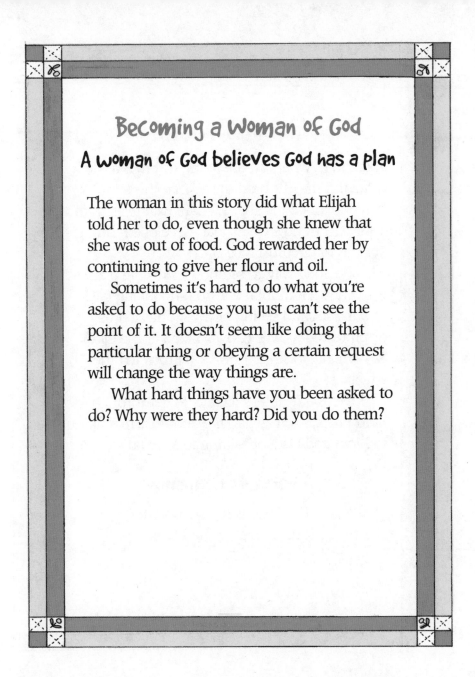

Becoming a Woman of God
A Woman of God believes God has a plan

The woman in this story did what Elijah told her to do, even though she knew that she was out of food. God rewarded her by continuing to give her flour and oil.

Sometimes it's hard to do what you're asked to do because you just can't see the point of it. It doesn't seem like doing that particular thing or obeying a certain request will change the way things are.

What hard things have you been asked to do? Why were they hard? Did you do them?

MoM'S TOUCH

Sometimes when we are going through a difficult time, it's hard to see that there is a bigger plan taking shape. Share examples from your past of how God's plan developed through a series of circumstances.

One good way to see how God's big plan is in constant motion is through looking back at our lives and seeing how God has led us or protected us. We can also look at the Old Testament stories of how God protected the Israelites.

Talk about different ways to get through hard times, such as praying about them, talking to Mom and Dad, or talking to a friend.

A Verse to Remember

The LORD is my shepherd;
I have everything I need.

Psalm 23:1

The kind woman from the little town of Shunem took great pride in the fact that her house was always neat and clean. She had enjoyed decorating her home and she loved sharing it with others. The little woman was known throughout Shunem for her hospitality and kindness.

The gentle woman was a good cook and generous hostess. The first time Elisha came to town she insisted that he stay at her home. She enjoyed having him as a guest. After all, he was a prophet of God. Soon Elisha had an invitation to stay at her home anytime.

After one of Elisha's visits, the gentle woman was cleaning the guest room when an interesting idea popped into her mind. Later that night she shared it with her husband. "Why don't we build on a room that will be for Elisha. Then any time he is in town he will know that he has a place to stay. He can even keep some of his things here if he wants."

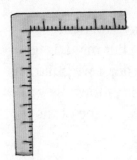

The woman's husband was surprised by her suggestion, but he was in favor of it. He made the plans immediately and the room was built and furnished before Elisha came back to town.

When Elisha knocked on her door a few weeks later, the woman welcomed him inside. She was so excited that she took his hand and pulled him through the house. "We have a surprise for you, Elisha. Look what we've made for you." Elisha was very happy. He thanked God for the kind woman and her generous husband.

Based on 2 Kings 4:8–11

Thank You, God

Becoming a Woman of God
A Woman of God is generous

This kind woman in Shunem generously shared what she had to help Elisha. God is pleased when we share what he gives us, especially when we use our belongings to help his workers.

There's always a big push to help people less fortunate during the Christmas holiday season. But people need help all year long.

In what ways can you give to others? Here are some ideas: sharing musical talent, preparing and serving food, fixing up houses, reading to older people. What else can you think of?

MoM'S ToUCH

Your children will learn generosity by watching you model it. Share ways you have been involved in generous giving, or ways that you have observed people being generous with their time and talents.

Comment on a time you observed your daughter being generous. Reinforce that characteristic in your daughter.

A Verse to Remember

Don't think only of your own good.
Think of other Christians
and what is best for them.

1 Corinthians 10:24

Good Advice for Naaman

The little girl was really very lucky. When she was captured she became a slave to the wife of Naaman. Mrs. Naaman was very kind to the little girl. In fact, in the little girl's secret heart of hearts she thought of Mrs. Naaman in place of her own mother whom she missed so much. She often talked with the older woman, telling her about her faith in God and how much she missed her family.

The little girl worked very hard for Mrs. Naaman and did her work cheerfully. One day when the little girl brought Mrs. Naaman's lunch to her, she found the older woman crying. "Why are you crying?" the girl asked. It was unusual that the woman would share her own feelings with the little girl, but she was so upset that they spilled out.

"I'm crying because my husband has leprosy. He has to leave home and live outside of town. I'm going to miss him very much."

The little girl was very sad. She liked Mr. Naaman, too. So she bravely said, "He doesn't have to leave. He can go see God's prophet, Elisha. I'm sure Elisha could help him."

The little girl seemed very sure that God would help Elisha heal Naaman. So Mrs. Naaman encouraged her husband to visit the prophet. But on the way Elisha's servant met him. "Elisha says you should go wash in the Jordan River seven times." Naaman was very angry that Elisha didn't speak to him personally, so he decided to just go home.

But back at Naaman's house the little girl prayed with all her heart that Mr. Naaman would see God's power. When Naaman did obey Elisha and was healed, the little girl danced with joy! She had helped the Naamans in two ways: Mr. Naaman's skin was healed, and both Mr. and Mrs. Naaman knew that God's power had healed him.

Based on 2 Kings 5:1–19

Becoming a Woman of God

A Woman of God can be a Child

This is a precious story in the Bible, because it shows us that even a child can lead people to God. Not only was this little girl a child, but she was also a slave. Her faith in God was so strong that she told Naaman God could heal him.

How can you share God's love with a friend? Maybe you could invite a friend to a Sunday school party or to a program at church. You could give a friend a book you like that has the message of God's love in it. Can you think of other ways to share God's love?

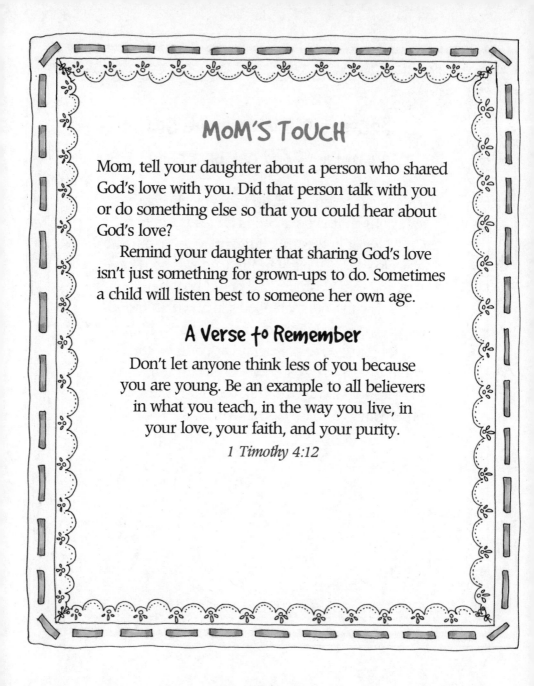

MOM'S TOUCH

Mom, tell your daughter about a person who shared God's love with you. Did that person talk with you or do something else so that you could hear about God's love?

Remind your daughter that sharing God's love isn't just something for grown-ups to do. Sometimes a child will listen best to someone her own age.

A Verse to Remember

Don't let anyone think less of you because
you are young. Be an example to all believers
in what you teach, in the way you live, in
your love, your faith, and your purity.

1 Timothy 4:12

"Esther, please help us. This may be the very reason God made you queen." Esther didn't want to hear what Mordecai was saying. She hadn't been much more than a child when she was chosen from hundreds of girls and made queen of Persia. Her great beauty and charm quickly won her the hearts of all who met her. But now the young queen was being tested.

Esther Wins a Beauty Contest

The problem started because Haman, a government leader, wanted everyone to bow down to him. One Jewish man, who happened to be Esther's uncle, refused to bow. Now Haman ordered that all the Jews in the land be killed!

"Mordecai, I can't help. No one, not even the king, knows that I'm Jewish. Remember, it was your idea for me to keep that a secret," Esther said.

"I know, dear, but all of us—including you—will die if we don't think of some way to stop Haman."

Esther went to her room and thought about the danger of going to the king when he hadn't called for her . . . he could have her killed. She wondered what he would think when he found out she was Jewish. She thought about all the dangers and choices. Then she sent a note to Mordecai: "I'm going to talk to the king. Pray for me—if I die, then I die."

Esther put on her prettiest dress and splashed on some perfume. Then she invited the king and Haman to a special dinner. They were enjoying the food and laughing and talking when Esther found the courage to say, "Haman is planning to kill me and my relatives!"

Haman nearly choked as Esther explained his whole evil plan and her own Jewishness. Esther breathed a deep sigh of relief as soldiers led Haman away. King Xerxes had him hung on the gallows which Haman had built to kill Mordecai. The Jews were saved, thanks to the courage of a beautiful, brave young queen.

Based on the Book of Esther

Becoming a Woman of God
A woman of God takes a stand for him

Wasn't Esther brave? The king could have ordered that she be killed because she came to him without being called—or because she was Jewish. Even if Esther was very scared, she knew she had to stop Haman.

Have you ever wanted to stand up for God when other kids were making fun of him? Have you ever heard kids saying mean things about someone else? Did you try to stop them? It's not easy to go against the crowd, is it?

MOM'S TOUCH

Share a story about some injustice that once bothered you (or currently troubles you), even if you have done nothing about it.

If you have taken a stand for God or another person, share that story. Were you scared? What was the outcome?

Discuss with your daughter that taking a stand for God might mean explaining why she goes to church or Sunday school. It might mean explaining why she prays before she eats lunch. Encourage her to give her explanations in gentleness and love. And remind her that she never has to take a stand alone—God will help her!

A Verse to Remember

For I can do everything
with the help of Christ who
gives me the strength I need.

Philippians 4:13

We're Having a Baby

ZECHARIAH

Elizabeth shook her head in frustration. "What are you trying to tell me? Why don't you just talk?"

Her husband, Zechariah, was just as frustrated as she was. Finally, he picked up a stick and wrote in the dirt, "We're going to have a baby."

Elizabeth read the words . . . then read them again. "A what? A baby? Do you know how old . . . have you lost your mind?"

Zechariah quickly scribbled another word in the dust: angel. At first Elizabeth didn't understand . . . it had been years since he had called her his "angel" so he must mean that he had seen an angel. Sure enough, through his scribbles Elizabeth learned that an angel had come to her husband and said that they would have a baby boy and that they must name him John.

Their son would prepare the world for the coming Messiah. What an honor! She also found out why Zechariah was drawing signs in the dust instead of telling her this miraculous news. He had doubted the angel's message so the messenger from God had taken his voice away until the baby was born. After hearing that, Elizabeth was careful not to question another bit of Zechariah's news.

At the oddest moments Elizabeth would rub her hand across her stomach and think, *A baby. I'm going to have a baby.* She and Zechariah had prayed for a child for years. But she had given up hope, thinking her withered old body was too old to carry a child. Joy bubbled up inside her as she thought, *Well, I surely won't argue with God about this.*

Nine months later, relatives gathered with Zechariah and Elizabeth to celebrate the birth of their son. Elizabeth cradled the child in her arms. Aunts and uncles argued back and forth with name ideas while Zechariah peeked over the crowd at Elizabeth. He raised a stone tablet in the air with big words scratched on it, "His name is John."

Based on Luke 1:5–25, 57–63

Becoming a Woman of God
A Woman of God enjoys God's surprises

Elizabeth and Zechariah must have thought their lives were all settled. They were old now and had never had children. Zechariah was busy with his work, and Elizabeth kept busy with the house and her friends.

Wow, did God give them a special surprise! He gave them a baby in their old age. When God is involved, nothing is impossible!

Is there something you have prayed about for a long, long time? What is it? Have you given up on God ever answering that prayer? Do you still pray for it?

MoM'S TOUCH

Help your daughter understand Elizabeth's emotions by explaining what it's like physically to have a child growing inside you. Maybe you, like Elizabeth, longed for a child but were unable to have one. Discuss with your daughter how God answered your prayer for a child.

Ask your daughter to describe the best surprise she ever received. Then tell her about a way God once surprised you. Spend a few minutes together in prayer, thanking God for his surprises.

A Verse to Remember

Keep on asking,
and you will be given what you ask for.
Keep on looking, and you will find.
Keep on knocking,
and the door will be opened.

Matthew 7:7

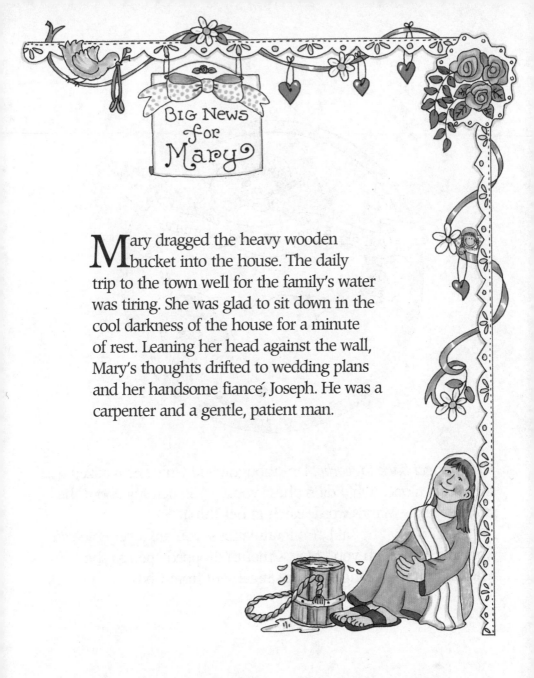

Big News for Mary

Mary dragged the heavy wooden bucket into the house. The daily trip to the town well for the family's water was tiring. She was glad to sit down in the cool darkness of the house for a minute of rest. Leaning her head against the wall, Mary's thoughts drifted to wedding plans and her handsome fiancé, Joseph. He was a carpenter and a gentle, patient man.

I'd better get back to work, Mary thought. Suddenly she realized that she wasn't alone. "Oh, I didn't hear you. . . ." Something about the stranger made Mary's words catch in her throat.

"Hello, Mary," he said. "Congratulations, you are a very blessed woman. God is with you." Mary's mouth dropped open as she realized that the stranger was an angel sent from God.

The angel continued speaking and Mary grew more frightened with each word he spoke. "Don't be afraid, Mary. I've come to tell you that you are going to have a baby." Mary backed away from the angel, until she bumped against the cold stone wall.

"I-I-I can't have a baby," she whispered. "I'm not even married . . ."

..God
Chose
me...?

"I know, but your baby will be God's son," the angel said. "You are to name him Jesus. His kingdom will never end!"

Mary's eyes grew as big as saucers and she nervously walked around the room. She had never felt so confused . . . or frightened . . . or honored. What would Joseph say? What would her family say? Had God really chosen her?

Mary stared into the angel's face and he waited for the incredible news to sink in before reminding her, "Nothing is impossible with God, Mary."

Mary closed her eyes and took a deep breath before saying, "I am God's servant. I will do whatever he wants me to do!" When she opened her eyes, the angel was gone.

Based on Luke 1:26–38

Becoming a Woman of God
A Woman of God is Chosen by God

Mary was chosen for a great honor. But God didn't choose her because she was pretty or because she sang well or because she was from the right family. He chose her because she loved God and wanted with all her heart to please him.

Have you ever been chosen for something? It feels good to be chosen for a team or chosen to be in a play. It feels good to be chosen for anything–especially if you know that you have earned the honor.

MoM'S ToUCH

Tell your daughter about a time you were chosen to do something or be in something. How did it feel to be chosen for this? Why were you chosen? Did it give you added responsibility? Were your friends happy for you or jealous of you?

Talk to your daughter about how God has chosen us to be his children. Talk about what it means to be in God's family.

A Verse to Remember

For his Holy Spirit
speaks to us deep in our hearts
and tells us that we are God's children.

Romans 8:16

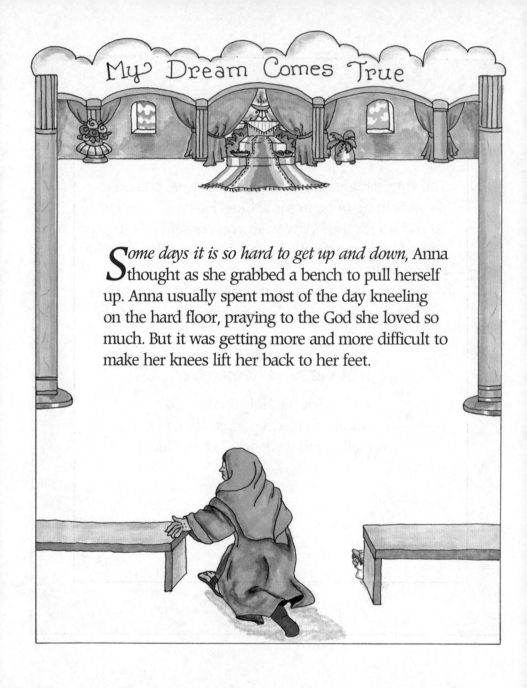

My Dream Comes True

Some days it is so hard to get up and down, Anna thought as she grabbed a bench to pull herself up. Anna usually spent most of the day kneeling on the hard floor, praying to the God she loved so much. But it was getting more and more difficult to make her knees lift her back to her feet.

Anna was getting up to check on her old friend, Simeon. She could hear him shouting. To Anna's old ears it sounded as if he were saying, "Praise God! Now I can die a happy man!" Anna had a lot of respect for Simeon. He spent a lot of time in the temple, as Anna did. She knew that he was a man of God. What on earth was he shouting about?

Anna stood still for a minute, catching her breath. Then she shuffled through the temple toward Simeon's voice. *There he is*, she thought. *He's holding a baby in his arms, a baby! Oh, be careful, you're lifting it so high into the air.* He was shouting, "Praise you, Lord. Just as you promised, I have seen the Savior of Israel, a light for the world! Now I can die a happy man."

Anna crept closer as Simeon gave the child back to his mother. *They must be here to dedicate the baby to God,* Anna thought. Just then she caught a glimpse of the baby's face. Anna's old heart skipped a beat. At that very moment God showed her that this baby was Messiah—the Savior that her people were waiting for.

Joy bubbled from deep inside Anna, spilling from her lips. "Praise God! Thank you for hearing the prayers of your people. Hallelujah!" Anna's wrinkled old body danced through the temple. She stopped every person she met and told them about the child. "The Savior has come. God has heard our prayers! Hallelujah!"

Based on Luke 2:25–38

Becoming a Woman of God
A Woman of God recognizes her Savior

It's been said that when a big herd of sheep is in the field and a shepherd calls, only the sheep that belong to him will come. That's because they recognize the voice of their shepherd.

When Anna saw baby Jesus, she immediately recognized that he was her Savior. Her heart was so in tune with God that she understood who this little baby was and what he would do when he grew up.

When you are in a crowd of people and your mom or dad calls your name, can you pick that single voice out of the noise? Do you recognize that voice, even with all the confusion? Does it make you feel good to know that mom or dad is there?

MOM'S TOUCH

Tell your daughter about the first time you knew Jesus was speaking to you. Were you a child? An adult?

Ask your daughter if she has heard Jesus call her. If she hasn't, explain to her how she can learn to hear and follow the Good Shepherd.

Point out that other people saw young Jesus and thought he was just another baby. But Anna and Simeon saw him and immediately knew who he was because in their hearts they were seeking to know God.

A Verse to Remember

My sheep recognize my voice;
I know them, and they follow me.
I give them eternal life,
and they will never perish.
No one will snatch them away from me.

John 10:27–28

My Son Is Lost

HAVE YOU SEEN ME?

JESUS

Mary's side hurt and her lungs felt as if they were going to burst, but she kept running. Joseph was three steps ahead of her as they raced back toward Jerusalem. *How on earth did we leave Jesus behind?* Mary silently screamed. *He's only twelve years old. What will happen to him?* She wished her feet would move faster.

Where could he be?

Jesus

"Joseph, this was supposed to be a happy time, it's the Passover . . . oh Joseph, what if we can't find him?" Mary cried to her husband.

Joseph waited for her to catch up with him. He hugged her tightly and said, "Trust God, Mary."

"I'm trying," Mary whispered, but her mother's heart cried, "I'm scared."

Mary filled with panic when she saw the crowds
in Jerusalem. *Why don't these people go home? We
have to find our son,* her heart cried. Mary and
Joseph ran up and down the streets of Jerusalem,
stopping people, describing Jesus . . . "He's about
so tall . . . gentle brown eyes. Have you seen him?
Please, help us." No one had seen him.

Three days later Mary was exhausted. She didn't think she would ever see Jesus again. "Let's go to the temple and pray for God's help," Joseph suggested. Mary went, but she felt numb inside, like part of her had died. She tried to pray, but the temple was buzzing with people talking about an amazing child who was actually teaching the teachers about God!

A child! It had to be Jesus! Mary and Joseph ran to where a crowd had gathered. Mary's heart flooded with relief when she saw Jesus. Through her sobs she said, "We looked everywhere for you. Why did you do this?"

Jesus was puzzled. "Didn't you know that I would be in my Father's house?" He went home with his parents then, and Mary couldn't stop touching his shoulder or brushing his hair back. *He's really here. He's safe*, her heart sang.

Based on Luke 2:41–52

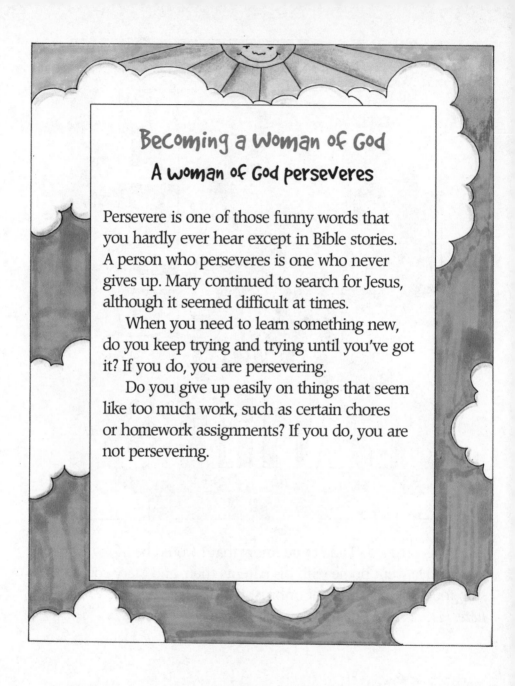

Becoming a Woman of God
A Woman of God perseveres

Persevere is one of those funny words that you hardly ever hear except in Bible stories. A person who perseveres is one who never gives up. Mary continued to search for Jesus, although it seemed difficult at times.

When you need to learn something new, do you keep trying and trying until you've got it? If you do, you are persevering.

Do you give up easily on things that seem like too much work, such as certain chores or homework assignments? If you do, you are not persevering.

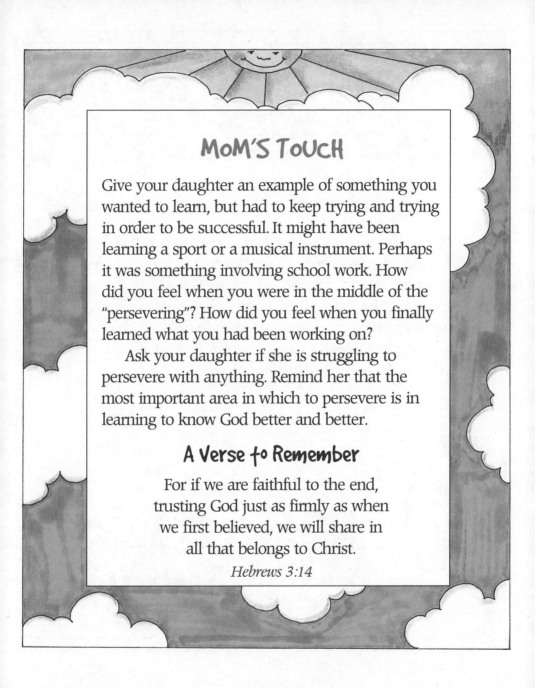

MoM'S ToUCH

Give your daughter an example of something you wanted to learn, but had to keep trying and trying in order to be successful. It might have been learning a sport or a musical instrument. Perhaps it was something involving school work. How did you feel when you were in the middle of the "persevering"? How did you feel when you finally learned what you had been working on?

Ask your daughter if she is struggling to persevere with anything. Remind her that the most important area in which to persevere is in learning to know God better and better.

A Verse to Remember

For if we are faithful to the end,
trusting God just as firmly as when
we first believed, we will share in
all that belongs to Christ.

Hebrews 3:14

Longing to Be Well

"I know he can help me. I've heard of the miracles he does in the name of God. But he's so busy—always surrounded by people who are begging him to do something for them," the sick woman sighed. Jesus and a crowd of people were coming down the road. *I don't want to bother Jesus. But I'm sure if I could just touch the hem of his robe, I'd be healed*, she thought.

"Yes"

I know He can help me.

"Well, I've got nothing to lose. The doctors can't help me, and I've been sick so long. This may be my last hope to get well." The woman wiggled and pushed her way through the crowd around Jesus. When she was near him, the woman quietly touched the bottom of Jesus' robe. Instantly she felt her body respond, like a flame shooting through her. "Ohh!" she cried, before clapping a hand over her mouth.

Jesus stopped suddenly and asked, "Who touched me?"

What is he talking about? his disciples wondered. There were hundreds of people around him. Fifty people probably brushed against him in the last five minutes.

But Jesus didn't let the matter drop. "Someone just touched me in order to be healed. I felt power leave me."

The woman shrank back into the crowd and listened to Jesus and his disciples talking. *Do I really think I can hide from him?* she thought. *He's God. I might as well speak up.* She meant to be brave, but when she stepped forward she started to shake. In a trembling voice, she said, "I touched you. I've been sick for twelve years and no one could help me. I just wanted to be well, and I knew that I would be if I just touched you."

When I touched your robe, I was healed....

The words rolled quickly from her. Everyone was quiet as the woman explained what she had done. But a ripple of shock ran through the crowd when she said, "When I touched your robe, I was healed."

Jesus smiled gently before saying, "Your faith has made you well, my child. Go live your life in peace."

Based on Mark 5:25–34

Becoming a Woman of God
A Woman of God steps out in faith

The woman in this story had a lot of faith. She believed Jesus was so powerful that she could be healed just by touching the hem of his robe. She knew that she didn't need him to touch her or pray for her or even speak to her.

Having faith means that you believe something is true even though you can't see it. When you sit down in a chair and expect it to hold you up and not let you crash to the floor, you are showing faith that the chair will do what it is supposed to do.

MoM'S Touch

Tell your daughter about a time when you stepped out in faith to try something. Perhaps your experience relates to a new job or moving to a new state. Tell her how you saw God working in the situation.

Do you or your daughter know anyone who has suffered a long illness, as the woman in the story did? Did that person get depressed and give up hope of ever being better? Discuss this with your daughter.

Encourage your daughter to have faith in God no matter what. We may miss many great blessings in life if we don't have faith in God.

A Verse to Remember

What is faith?
It is the confident assurance that
what we hope for is going to happen.
It is the evidence of things we cannot yet see.

Hebrews 11:1

PAY to the Order of God

Giving My All

$ ♡♡♡

Faithful

Praise Him!

The shriveled little woman stood behind a pillar in the temple. She watched as people put their money in the offering box and prayed to God. *This is a holy time*, she thought. *It's a time to praise God for all he has given me.* That was an interesting thought, coming from a woman whose husband was dead and who barely had two coins to rub together. Often she didn't even know where her next meal was coming from.

The woman didn't have much family left; most of her loved ones had died. The one most important thing in her life was God. She came to the temple every day to worship and praise him. Now she got in line to give her offering to God. The man ahead of her was dressed in a nice robe with fancy fringe around the edges. He was a rich man who surely had much to be thankful for.

The woman waited with her head bowed. The man made a big show of putting his offering in the box. He made sure everyone was watching. It sounded like a lot of money clinking into the box. The man prayed loudly, but the woman was shocked when she heard him. He didn't praise God at all. Instead, he told God how wonderful he was and how lucky God was that he loved God.

When it was her turn, the poor widow dropped two small coins into the offering box. They didn't make much noise. The two coins together were barely worth a penny. After she put them in the box, the woman bowed her head and praised God for his many wonderful gifts to her. She prayed that her offering would be used to help those who were poorer and needier than she.

The woman didn't notice the rich men standing nearby who were laughing at her. "What a worthless offering. It isn't worth the space it takes up in the box." Just then the woman looked up and saw Jesus standing across the room. He looked deep into the woman's eyes. Jesus knew that this poor woman had given everything she had to God's work. She could see the approval in his eyes. The woman's heart filled with praise and love for God.

Based on Mark 12:41–44

Becoming a Woman of God
A Woman of God is humble

The poor woman was very generous. She gave all that she had to God's work. She knew that it was important to help the needy, and she was willing to give everything for that purpose.

This woman was also very humble. That means that she didn't think more of herself than she should.

Are you humble? Do you know people who are constantly telling everyone how smart they are or how good they are at sports? Do you enjoy being around people who brag about themselves?

MOM'S TOUCH

Tell your daughter about a humble person you have known. Perhaps you have known a missionary who was willing to live in very humble circumstances in order to share God's love with people.

Point out that a humble person doesn't have to own the best of everything, but is happy with what she has. She is willing, as the woman in this story, to give her money, time, talents, and energy to the poor. A humble person knows that all she has are gifts from God, so she happily gives back to him.

A Verse to Remember

Don't be selfish;
don't live to make a
good impression on others.
Be humble, thinking of others
as better than yourself.

Philippians 2:3

The Gift of Life

"O God, why did you take my son?—my only son?" When her son first got sick the worried mom prayed with all her heart, but the boy still died. The pain in the mother's heart was so great that she could feel nothing else. Her heart was numb. "God, first you took my husband, now my son. It hurts so much. Where are you, God? Where are you?"

Somehow the boy's funeral was planned. She wasn't sure how. She lived from day to day in a fog, hardly aware that friends were around her, or that they were doing things for her. She was grateful for their help, but couldn't even tell them how much it meant to her.

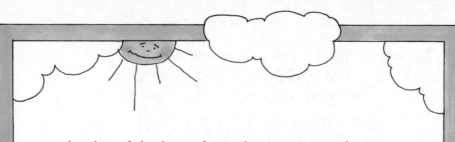

The day of the boy's funeral was warm and sunny, but the heartbroken mother didn't notice the sunshine or feel its warmth on her skin. The funeral procession walked through the town gate and toward the cemetery outside of town. Right outside the gate they met a group of men who had to wait for the procession to pass so they could go into town.

The mother walked slowly behind her son's coffin, her friends trying to comfort her. Suddenly a man's voice said, "Don't cry." The mourners looked at the man as if he were crazy. How could he tell the heartbroken mother not to cry?

The gentle man laid his hand on the boy's coffin. "Young man," he said, "get up!"

Everyone watched as the mother stared at the man in disbelief. When her son sat up, she grabbed her chest, struggling to breathe. Then the grateful woman hugged her son—her only son. She looked up . . . into the face of Jesus—God's only Son, and with tears running down her face she praised God for his wonderful love and for giving her back her son.

Based on Luke 7:11–17

Becoming a Woman of God

A Woman of God thanks God for sending Jesus

This mother whose only son had died may have understood more than most people how much God loves us. God sent his only Son to earth to die for our sins so that we can live in heaven with him one day. That is an awesome gift!

Has anyone you loved ever died? Who was it? How did you feel?

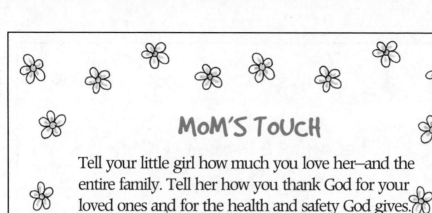

MOM'S TOUCH

Tell your little girl how much you love her—and the entire family. Tell her how you thank God for your loved ones and for the health and safety God gives.

If your family has lost a loved one, talk about the experience. If that loved one was a Christian, reinforce that you will see her or him again one day—in heaven!

Ask your daughter if she has asked Jesus to come into her heart. If she hasn't, guide her through the steps of admitting she has sinned, asking forgiveness for her sins, and thanking God for sending Jesus to die for her sins. Then encourage her to ask Jesus to come live in her heart forever.

A Verse to Remember

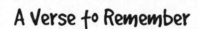

For God so loved the world that he gave his only Son, so that everyone who believes in him will not perish but have eternal life.

John 3:16

"Don't worry, Sweetheart. Everything is going to be OK," Jairus told his daughter. The little girl adored her daddy and believed he could fix anything. For all her twelve years, he had taken care of every problem she ever had. Then one day she got very sick. The little girl was confused because it was the first time her wonderful dad couldn't make everything right.

Daddy's Girl

I Love You

DADDY

God Bless You

Her daddy said not to worry. He had heard of a man named Jesus who did wonderful miracles—he healed sick people, and he even brought dead people back to life. Her daddy said he would get Jesus, so she should just rest and wait for him to come back. The little girl believed her daddy because he always did what he said he would do.

She laid back in her bed and rested, confident that
her daddy would be back soon with Jesus. She waited
and waited, all the while getting sicker and sicker.
Her momma stayed beside her and prayed for God
to make her well. The little girl tried to hang on. She
knew that her daddy would soon be back. But before
her daddy could return, the little girl died.

HAVE FAITH IN JESUS

The little girl's momma and grandparents
cried and a servant ran to tell Jairus that
it was too late—his precious little girl
was dead. When Jairus heard the news,
he sadly turned and started home. But
Jesus insisted on coming with him, even
though the girl was dead.

Later, Jairus held his little girl and told her how people had laughed when Jesus said she wasn't dead, but that she was just sleeping. But then Jesus had taken her hand and said, "Get up, little girl," and she did!

The little girl loved hearing the story and asked to hear it over and over again. Jairus always ended the story by hugging her and thanking God for giving his daughter back to him.

Based on Mark 5:22–24, 35–43

Becoming a Woman of God

A Woman of God thanks God for second chances

Jairus's daughter was given a second chance at life. If you were Jairus's daughter wouldn't you want to hear the story over and over? That experience may have changed how she looked at life.

Have you ever been given a second chance? Maybe when you disobeyed, Mom and Dad forgave you and gave you a second chance. What about at school? Maybe you did poorly on a test, and you were given a chance to retake it.

Life is filled with second chances. A wise person understands that and makes the most of the second chance.

Mom's Touch

How do you feel when your daughter disobeys? How about when she breaks the same rule over and over? Share your feelings with your daughter.

Can you remember a time when you were given a second chance at something? How did you respond? Explain to your daughter how you felt about the person who gave you the second chance.

Ask your daughter how she feels when you give her a second chance. Remind her that God will give us a second chance when we confess our sins and ask for his forgiveness.

A Verse to Remember

If we confess our sins to him,
he is faithful and just to forgive us
and to cleanse us from every wrong.

1 John 1:9

A Gracious Hostess

All through Martha's childhood her mother said she was a worrier. Martha couldn't help it. She worried and fussed because everything had to be perfect . . . especially when they had company. There couldn't be a speck of dust in the whole house, the table had to be set beautifully with fresh flowers, and dinner had to be ready exactly on time. Martha simply couldn't settle for anything less.

There couldn't be two more opposite people than Martha and her sister. Martha was a "doer" while Mary was a "thinker." Mary could be gone for hours, smelling flowers, watching birds, or chatting with merchants. When they had guests for dinner, Mary got so involved in talking to them that she'd forget to help Martha serve the meal. This wasn't a problem for Mary, but Martha was often very frustrated with her sister.

When the sisters heard that Jesus was coming to visit, there was a flurry of busyness . . . from Martha. She cleaned and cooked and washed and worked right up to the minute Jesus came. Martha made a wonderful dinner, and she thought Mary would surely help with the final preparations. But as soon as Jesus came in, Mary sat down right at his feet to listen to his wonderful stories. Martha stomped off to the kitchen in a huff.

Martha scurried around the kitchen, mixing, stirring, and chopping. Every few minutes she peeked around the door, hoping Mary was coming to help. She wasn't. In fact, each time Martha looked, Mary seemed to be deeper in conversation with Jesus. Pretty soon, Martha was steaming mad. *I work my fingers to the bone to clean the house and prepare a wonderful dinner and Mary just sits out there talking to him*, she thought. *It isn't fair!*

Martha was so angry that she began slamming things around the kitchen. Finally, she could take it no longer. Marching in to Jesus, she said, "Tell her to get up and help me. I'd like to hear your stories, too, but someone has to cook dinner."

Jesus was surprised at Martha's anger. Mary didn't dare say a word, but Jesus said, "Martha, you're so upset about your work. But, Mary knows that talking to me is more important than anything. Forget the kitchen; let's talk."

Based on Luke 10:38–42

Becoming a Woman of God

A Woman of God knows what's most important

Martha had good intentions. After all, she was busy doing what she was good at. It was important to her to have the house clean for Jesus' visit and to serve him a good meal.

But, even though she meant well, Martha let her work keep her so busy that she missed the most important thing—spending time with Jesus.

Nothing should be more important than spending time with Jesus. Even if God has given you some special talents that you can use in church, such as singing or playing an instrument, those talents should never get in the way of spending time with God.

MoM'S TOUCH

Have you ever gotten so busy "doing things" that you let slide the really important things in life? Things like spending time daily with God, or spending time with your family? It's easy for that to happen in our busy world. Talk to your daughter about your struggle between the "urgent" and the "important."

Tell her some ways you try to make room for what's really important. Then help her plan a daily schedule that includes quiet time with God.

A Verse to Remember

Love the LORD your God,
walk in all his ways, obey his commands,
be faithful to him, and serve him with
all your heart and all your soul.

Joshua 22:5

Lazarus, Come Out!

Mary choked back tears as she poured spices on Lazarus's body. Martha was doing most of the work to prepare their brother for burial. She didn't act sad at all, but Mary knew she was. Working hard was Martha's way of handling her pain. Suddenly, Mary felt tired. She sat down and thought back to when she, Martha, and Lazarus were children.

A smile tugged at Mary's mouth as she remembered how Lazarus loved to tease. "Mary, I know it's hard, but we must finish," Martha gently interrupted.

"Aren't you tired, Martha?" Mary asked.

"Yes, I am tired . . . and disappointed that Jesus didn't come," Martha sighed. "He could have helped Lazarus. There, I've said it."

Mary sighed. She was disappointed, too.

The sisters had sent for Jesus when Lazarus had gotten sick. They were sure he would come and heal their brother. But he didn't, and Lazarus had died.

After Lazarus was buried, Mary and Martha went home. Many relatives and friends came to comfort them. A few days later someone shouted, "Jesus is coming!"

Martha dropped the dough she was kneading and ran to meet him. "My brother is dead," she told him. "If you had come when we sent for you, he would still be alive."

"Martha, those who believe in me are given eternal life. They will never die. Do you believe that?"

"Yes," Martha said, "I know you are the Son of God."

Mary came to see Jesus, too. She also said that Lazarus would have lived if Jesus had come sooner. She could barely speak through her choking sobs.

"Where is Lazarus buried?" Jesus asked. Tears were crawling down his face, too. Mary and Martha showed him the tomb, a cave with a big stone covering the opening.

"Move the stone," Jesus ordered. Martha was shocked. "No, the smell will be awful. He has been dead four days!"

"Watch what God will do," Jesus answered. Martha grabbed Mary's hand, and they watched Jesus. He looked up and prayed. Then he called, "Lazarus, come out!" Mary closed her eyes, but Martha didn't. When Martha gasped and squeezed her hand, Mary opened one eye. A man was standing in the cave's door, wrapped in graveclothes. Lazarus was alive!

Based on John 11:1–45

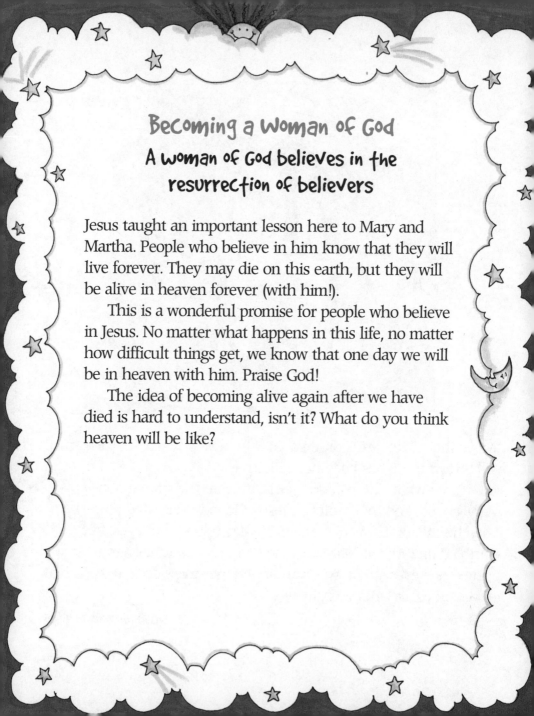

Becoming a Woman of God
A Woman of God believes in the resurrection of believers

Jesus taught an important lesson here to Mary and Martha. People who believe in him know that they will live forever. They may die on this earth, but they will be alive in heaven forever (with him!).

This is a wonderful promise for people who believe in Jesus. No matter what happens in this life, no matter how difficult things get, we know that one day we will be in heaven with him. Praise God!

The idea of becoming alive again after we have died is hard to understand, isn't it? What do you think heaven will be like?

MOM'S TOUCH

Share with your daughter what you know about heaven. Talk about how you feel when you think about seeing loved ones there who have already died.

Explain how this promise is one of the reasons there is an urgency to share God's love with all those around you. We all want our friends and family members to be with us in heaven someday.

Discuss someone you and your daughter both know who doesn't know about Jesus. Can you think of a way to share God's love with that person?

A Verse to Remember

I am the resurrection and the life.
Those who believe in me,
even though they die
like everyone else, will live again.

John 11:25

Miracle of Mud

She was his mother. If she could have changed things, she would have. When her son was born blind, of course she prayed, "Take my eyesight, just let my son see." She tried everything that doctors suggested. She wondered what she could have done differently when she was pregnant or even if he was blind because of a sin she or her husband had committed. But he remained blind. Now he was a blind man who could only beg to earn his living.

One afternoon a crowd of Pharisees showed up, dragging her son with them. Someone shouted, "Is this your son? Wasn't he born blind?" She started to answer, but he shouted again, "How come he can see now?"

Her heart leaped into her throat. *He can see? After all these years, he can see?* She looked at her son and realized that he was seeing her—for the very first time.

She wanted to hug him, ask him what happened, but the Pharisees kept shouting, "Why can he see now?"

Her husband came out and together they faced the crowd. "Yes, this is our son. Yes, he was born blind. We don't know why he can see now. He's an adult; ask him."

The confused parents listened as their son explained, "Jesus spit on the ground and made mud. Then he smeared the mud on my eyes. I didn't know what he was doing, but when he told me to wash off the mud in the pool of Siloam, I did. As soon as I did, I could see!"

Peek-a-boo

The worried mother twisted her scarf in her hands. *Son*, she thought, *be careful; these men don't like Jesus. They'll be angry that you're giving him credit for this.* The Pharisees leaned right into her son's face. She wanted to yank them back, but they kept asking, "How did he heal you?"

"Why do you keep asking me?" her son sighed. "I told you everything he did!"

Oh my, she worried, *they're going to throw him in jail.* But just then Jesus himself walked up. She couldn't take her eyes off Jesus. He was a gentle man, but somehow power and authority flowed from him. He turned to her son and asked, "Do you believe in the Son of Man?"

The woman's heart sang as she saw her grown-up son fall to his knees and worship Jesus. "I believe," he said.

Based on John 9:1–41

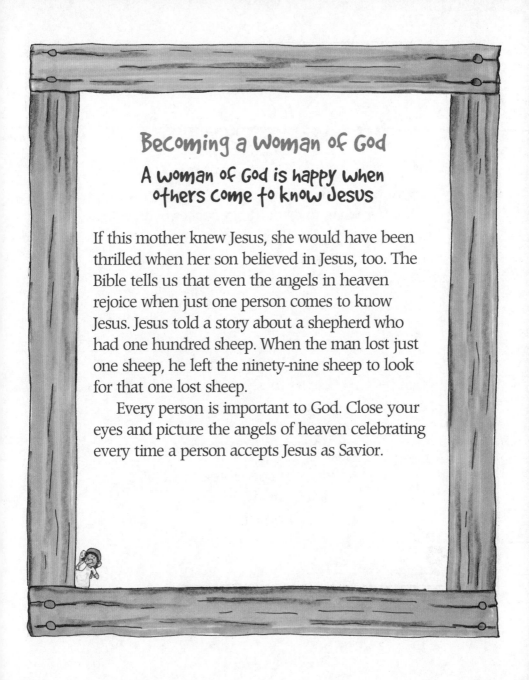

Becoming a Woman of God

A Woman of God is happy when others come to know Jesus

If this mother knew Jesus, she would have been thrilled when her son believed in Jesus, too. The Bible tells us that even the angels in heaven rejoice when just one person comes to know Jesus. Jesus told a story about a shepherd who had one hundred sheep. When the man lost just one sheep, he left the ninety-nine sheep to look for that one lost sheep.

Every person is important to God. Close your eyes and picture the angels of heaven celebrating every time a person accepts Jesus as Savior.

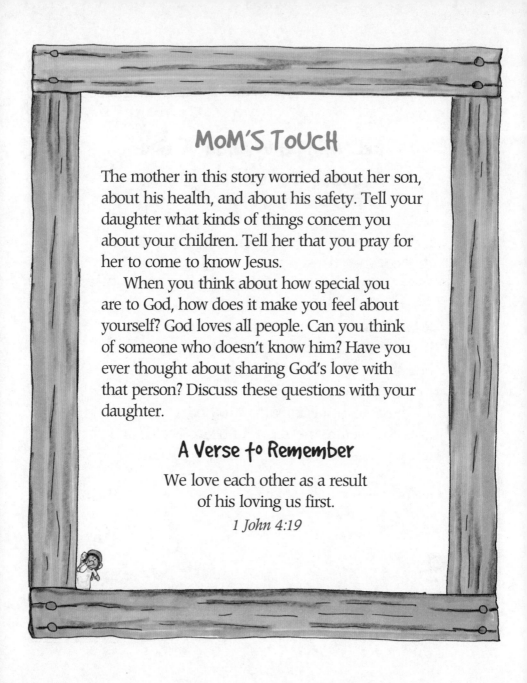

MOM'S TOUCH

The mother in this story worried about her son, about his health, and about his safety. Tell your daughter what kinds of things concern you about your children. Tell her that you pray for her to come to know Jesus.

When you think about how special you are to God, how does it make you feel about yourself? God loves all people. Can you think of someone who doesn't know him? Have you ever thought about sharing God's love with that person? Discuss these questions with your daughter.

A Verse to Remember

We love each other as a result
of his loving us first.

1 John 4:19

The woman stood across the street watching men go into Simon's house. When it seemed that all of Simon's guests had arrived, the woman crept a little closer and peeked in an open window. The wonderful smell of expensive food drifted out, finer food than she had ever eaten. The men in the room were talking and laughing.

Her eyes roamed through the room until she found the one face for which she was searching. Jesus. The woman dared to lean even closer for a better look at him. Her heart filled with love for this gentle man. She had met him once before, and he had chased away the demons that haunted her days and nights, giving her a chance for a normal life.

The woman was so overwhelmed with love for Jesus that she did something many would consider foolish. Hurrying to her shabby home she took a beautiful alabastar jar from her cupboard. It was filled with priceless perfume, more special than anything else she owned and worth more money than all her other possessions put together. She was going to give it away.

She wrapped the priceless jar in a cloth and hurried back
to Simon's house. She wasn't welcome in his home because
most people didn't approve of her lifestyle. The woman
stopped at the door and took a deep breath before barging
in. She went to Jesus and knelt at his feet.

The room became very quiet as the men watched tears
run down the woman's face and fall on Jesus' feet. She
gently wiped them away with her hair.

A loud gasp rolled through the room when she broke open the jar and poured the priceless perfume on Jesus' feet.

Simon criticized Jesus for letting such a woman touch him, but the woman's heart filled with love for Jesus when he defended her. She had so much to be thankful for because Jesus had forgiven her for so much.

Now he gently lifted her to her feet and said, "Your faith has saved you; go in peace."

Based on Luke 7:36–50

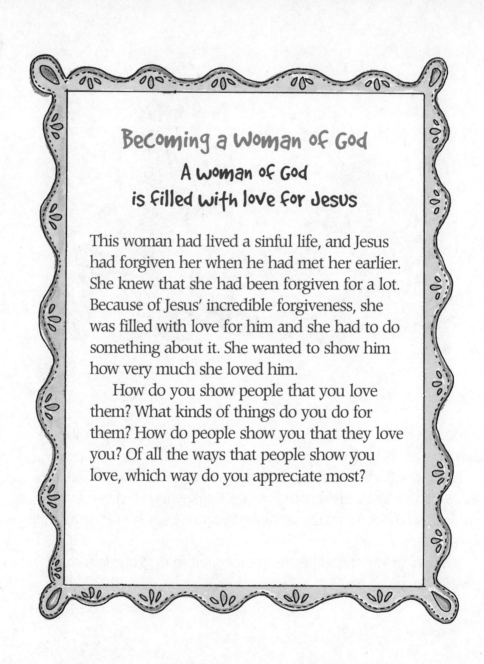

Becoming a Woman of God
A Woman of God
is filled with love for Jesus

This woman had lived a sinful life, and Jesus had forgiven her when he had met her earlier. She knew that she had been forgiven for a lot. Because of Jesus' incredible forgiveness, she was filled with love for him and she had to do something about it. She wanted to show him how very much she loved him.

How do you show people that you love them? What kinds of things do you do for them? How do people show you that they love you? Of all the ways that people show you love, which way do you appreciate most?

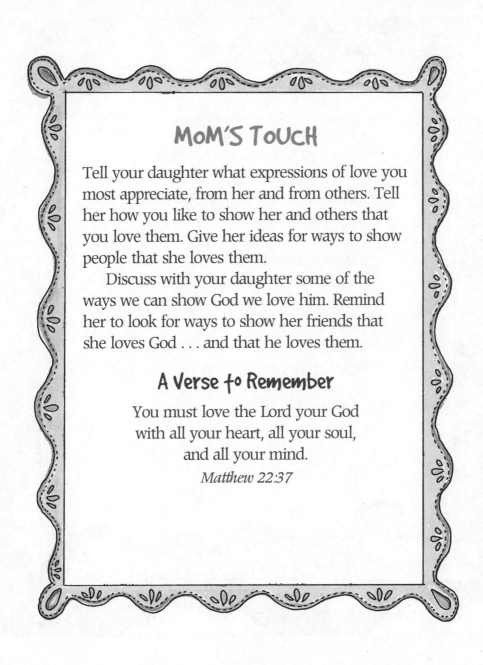

MOM'S TOUCH

Tell your daughter what expressions of love you most appreciate, from her and from others. Tell her how you like to show her and others that you love them. Give her ideas for ways to show people that she loves them.

Discuss with your daughter some of the ways we can show God we love him. Remind her to look for ways to show her friends that she loves God . . . and that he loves them.

A Verse to Remember

You must love the Lord your God
with all your heart, all your soul,
and all your mind.

Matthew 22:37

Sometimes late at night Mary would look at the twinkling stars and recall when the shepherds and wise men had come to worship her child. She remembered old Simeon and Anna in the temple saying her baby was the Savior of the world . . . the Messiah. Mary knew the teachings about the Messiah. But when people said those things about Jesus, she tucked them away deep in her heart and wondered what they all meant.

A Mother's Broken Heart

Today, she knew what they meant . . . and her heart was breaking. With every ounce of her being, Mary wanted to run through the streets of Jerusalem shouting, "Don't hurt him. He's my son. God, do something—STOP THEM!" Yet deep in her heart, she knew that the events of this day could not be stopped. Mary stood in the crowd as Jesus struggled to carry the heavy wooden cross. The cross on which he would die.

Mary was swept along with the crowd to the hill called Golgotha. She slid to the back of the crowd when the soldiers threw Jesus to the ground and began pounding the heavy spikes through his hands and feet and into the wooden cross. With every clank of the hammer, Mary wanted to turn and run as far away from this horrible scene as possible, but she couldn't. He was her son, and she had to stay with him.

When the cross was dropped into the ground, Mary looked up at Jesus. Blood was running down his face, mixed with the sweat of agonizing pain. She looked into his eyes, the same eyes she had played hide and seek with when he was a toddler, eyes that had laughingly teased her when he was a child, gentle eyes that even on this most horrible of days were filled with love for the sinful people who had come to watch him die.

Mary's eyes were locked on Jesus; she wished she could send strength from her body to his. She knew the end was near when Jesus asked one of his friends to take care of her and she felt an arm slip around her shoulder.

When Jesus died, Mary fell to her knees, sobbing in agony. "My arms feel so empty; I ache to hold my son, to tell him that everything will be alright." Simeon's long ago words made sense now. Her soul was pierced by the pain of this moment.

Based on John 19:1–30

Becoming a Woman of God
A Woman of God
understands Jesus' sacrifice

On the day that Jesus died, Mary was very sad. It wasn't fair that the Son of God and the Savior of the world was dying on a cross. It made Mary's heart break. It might have been easy for Mary to forget that this horrible moment was part of God's big plan to save mankind.

Jesus left heaven to come to earth and live as a poor man. He was treated badly by the very people he came to save. And he was killed as if he were a murderer. He did all of this because of his great love for us.

How do you feel when you are blamed for something you did not do?

MoM'S TOUCH

There isn't an emotion much more intense than a mother's love. Tell your daughter about a time when she was sick or hurting and you hurt right along with her.

In the Old Testament, people had to sacrifice an animal, such as a sheep, to God in order to ask for the forgiveness of their sins.

Talk to your daughter about what Jesus went through because he loved us. Jesus' death on the cross is the sacrifice for our sin. When we confess our sins and accept Jesus' sacrifice, he will come and live in our hearts forever.

A Verse to Remember

Believe on the Lord Jesus
and you will be saved.

Acts 16:31

A New Day Dawns

The three women got up early Sunday morning, before the sun rose. Their hearts were heavy with pain. The man they had believed in with all their hearts was gone . . . dead. Each of the women was lost in her own thoughts: *I thought he was the one—the Messiah. How can he be dead? I kept waiting for him to call an army of angels to rescue him from that horrible cross, but he didn't. He didn't. And now he's dead.*

Even in the middle of their pain and confusion the women wanted to do what was right. So they gathered spices and perfumes to put on his body. It was their custom to do this after a person had died. But there hadn't been time on the day he died because it was too close to the Sabbath. At first the women walked along in silence, each lost in her own sad thoughts.

How can we move it?

But as they neared the tomb, one woman spoke. Her practical question broke through the fog of grief surrounding each of them. "How are we going to move the stone?" The women stopped and looked at each other. It was overwhelming. They had been through so much in the last few days and they were exhausted. "How are we going to move the huge stone that covers the tomb door?" The woman repeated her question.

The women were still worried about the stone when they reached the cave. Then the first woman shouted, "It's gone. The stone is gone—the tomb is open!" They stared at the gaping doorway, more confused than ever.

Suddenly, an angel stood in front of them. "I know you're looking for Jesus," the angel said. "He isn't here. He came back to life, just as he said he would. Hurry to town and tell his friends."

For a split second the women stood in silence, letting the angel's news sink in. Then they exploded with joy. They went from deep, deep pain to incredible joy so quickly that their hearts had trouble keeping up. "He's alive!" they shouted, running to the disciples. "He's alive. Just as he said, he has come back to life!"

Based on Luke 24:1–12

Becoming a Woman of God
A Woman of God has hope

These women thought all hope was gone.
They thought all their hope had died with
Jesus. So the angel's announcement that Jesus
was alive again brought hope back to their
hearts.

Hope helps us through the hard times. If
we believe that Jesus is alive, we share the
same hope that the women in this story had.

Have you ever hoped for something? What
was it? Did it happen? How did you feel then?

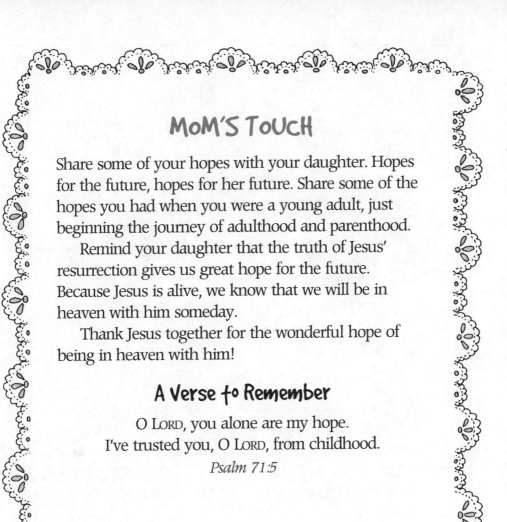

MOM'S TOUCH

Share some of your hopes with your daughter. Hopes for the future, hopes for her future. Share some of the hopes you had when you were a young adult, just beginning the journey of adulthood and parenthood.

Remind your daughter that the truth of Jesus' resurrection gives us great hope for the future. Because Jesus is alive, we know that we will be in heaven with him someday.

Thank Jesus together for the wonderful hope of being in heaven with him!

A Verse to Remember

O LORD, you alone are my hope.
I've trusted you, O LORD, from childhood.

Psalm 71:5

Mary Magdalene couldn't leave. The disciples had gone back to town, convinced that Jesus had risen from the dead. But Mary couldn't bring herself to leave the tomb. It was all too confusing. Had he really come back to life? If not, where was his body? Had someone stolen it as a cruel joke?

When Jesus died on Friday, it was the darkest day of Mary's life. He was such a pure and holy man and she didn't understand why anyone would hurt him. She wanted more than anything to believe that he was truly alive. But there had been so many disappointments in the last few days, she was afraid to believe this time. So she sat beside the tomb, crying. After a while, she ducked inside the tomb for one last lonely look around.

The cave suddenly filled with light and Mary looked up to see two beautiful angels. "Why are you crying?" they asked.

"Because someone has taken Jesus away, and I don't know where he is," she said. The angels left and Mary came out into the sunlight feeling an unbearable sense of loss.

Sinking down on a rock, Mary thought about things she wished she had told him. Jesus had forgiven her when she hadn't been able to forgive herself. *I wish I had another chance to tell him how much that meant,* she thought.

As Mary started to leave, she saw a man standing nearby. "Sir, are you the gardener? Did you take Jesus' body away?" Words spilled from Mary's lips. "Tell me where you put him. I'll get him."

"Mary."

Wait, something was familiar. Mary stared at the man until the fog in her brain lifted and she realized, "It's Jesus!" Bursting into tears she rushed to hug him and whisper all the words that had been flooding her heart.

But Jesus gently stopped her. "You can't touch me yet, Mary. Tell my friends that I'm going back to my Father—to your Father." Mary cried with joy as she left for town, knowing that everything would be all right now.

Based on John 20:10–18

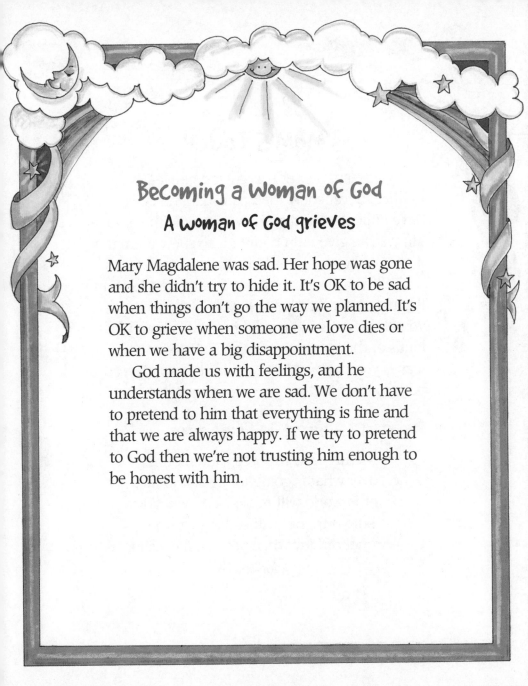

Becoming a Woman of God
A Woman of God grieves

Mary Magdalene was sad. Her hope was gone and she didn't try to hide it. It's OK to be sad when things don't go the way we planned. It's OK to grieve when someone we love dies or when we have a big disappointment.

God made us with feelings, and he understands when we are sad. We don't have to pretend to him that everything is fine and that we are always happy. If we try to pretend to God then we're not trusting him enough to be honest with him.

MoM'S TOUCH

Has your daughter ever seen you grieve? If mothers never show their pain, daughters will have difficulty learning how to handle theirs. One gift we can give our children is to show them that it's OK to be sad. Even Jesus was sad sometimes.

Tell your daughter about a sad time you went through. How did God help you? Ask her to tell you about one of her sad times. Talk about what kinds of things make you sad. Talk about what makes you happy. Mary Magdalene experienced both sadness and joy very close together!

A Verse to Remember

Truly, you will weep and mourn
over what is going to happen to me,
but the world will rejoice. You will grieve,
but your grief will suddenly turn to
wonderful joy when you see me again.

John 16:20

A Generous Seamstress

Dorcas

Nothing gave Dorcas greater joy than helping someone who was poor. She wasn't a great cook, or a wonderful teacher, but one thing she was good at was sewing. She loved to make pretty, warm clothes for people. Dorcas knew that when a poor woman put on a new dress or coat, she felt better about herself. So Dorcas was always sewing for someone.

When Dorcas started feeling sick, her friends tried to get her to slow down. "Take some time off. You've earned it. Take a rest," they told her. But Dorcas kept stitching away. There was always one more person who could use a new robe or dress. Dorcas wouldn't let herself slow down.

Her friends noticed that Dorcas was getting weaker and weaker. Her stitches weren't as even as before and her fingers weren't flying across the fabric. "Please, Dorcas, stop and rest," they pleaded.

But she wouldn't. "The good Lord gave me a gift, and I'm going to use it." A few days later, Dorcas's friends found her dead, with her sewing needle still in her hands.

Dorcas's friends cried as they put perfumes on her body and dressed her in a nice dress. It was sad that such a giving person was gone. Many people would miss her.

Then someone mentioned that Peter was nearby. "God has helped Peter do wonderful miracles. He has even raised people from the dead," someone added. "Let's send for him. Maybe he will help Dorcas!"

FABRIC BOX

When Peter came, Dorcas's friends sadly showed him the clothing she had made for them. Peter sent them all out of the room. Then he prayed and took Dorcas by the hand. "Get up," he ordered. Her eyes fluttered open and breath swooshed back into her body. Dorcas sat up, alive and well! Peter called her friends to come back in. They all joyfully praised God for giving Dorcas back to them.

Based on Acts 9:36–43

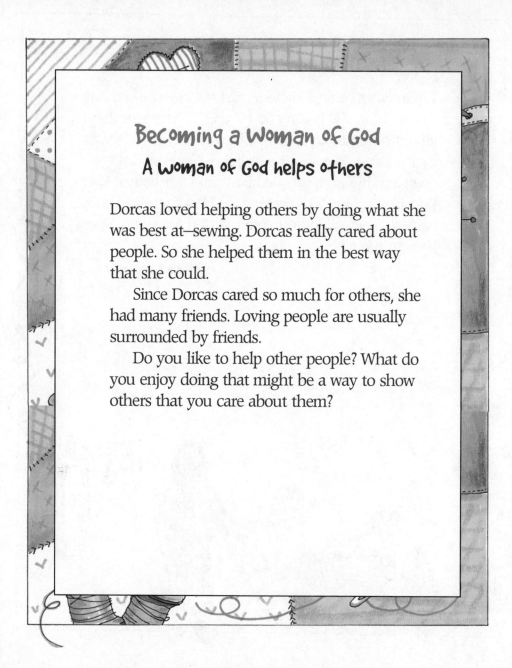

Becoming a Woman of God
A Woman of God helps others

Dorcas loved helping others by doing what she was best at—sewing. Dorcas really cared about people. So she helped them in the best way that she could.

Since Dorcas cared so much for others, she had many friends. Loving people are usually surrounded by friends.

Do you like to help other people? What do you enjoy doing that might be a way to show others that you care about them?

MOM'S TOUCH

Discuss with your daughter a time when someone helped you in some way. What did that person do for you? Did it make you feel as if that person cared about you?

Think out loud with your daughter about ways that the two of you can help others. What do you both enjoy doing? How can you show people that you care about them?

A Verse to Remember

This is the message
we have heard from the beginning:
We should love one another.

1 John 3:11

Lydia's days were busy with selling the purple dye for which her hometown of Thyatira was famous. The business was going well and she was thankful that she didn't have to worry about money or food. When the Sabbath came, she could have used the time to rest. After all, she wasn't Jewish. But, on the Sabbath day Lydia would gather with a small group of women on the banks of the river outside town.

One bright Sabbath morning, the women had gathered on the quiet riverbanks when a man's voice interrupted their conversation. Lydia looked up at the two men and was shocked to recognize the apostle Paul. He traveled all around the country teaching people about God. *What is Paul doing here, on a damp riverbank with a bunch of women?* she thought. It wasn't long before Lydia knew.

Paul sat down with the women. He prayed with them and began teaching them about Jesus' death and resurrection and God's incredible plan. Lydia listened as Paul explained God's wonderful love. She had worshiped God but had never really understood him until now. It seemed to Lydia as if God opened a window in her heart for just a moment, and, suddenly everything made sense.

Joyfully, Lydia asked Jesus to be her Lord and Savior. "Would you baptize me right now?" she asked Paul. They stepped into the river and Lydia said she believed in Jesus. Then Paul lowered her down into the water. When he lifted her out of the water, Lydia knew in her heart that she was a new person and her life would never be the same.

Lydia wanted to run into town and tell everyone, to shout her new faith from the rooftops. She was also eager to share all that she had. Turning to Paul, Lydia said, "You must come stay at my house. Please, bring your friends. I have plenty of room. If you really believe that I'm a Christian now, please come." Paul laughed at Lydia's enthusiasm and happily accepted her hospitality.

Based on Acts 16:11–15

Becoming a Woman of God
A Woman of God is God's Friend

Lydia was introduced to a personal relationship with God by the apostle Paul. As soon as she met God, what did she want to do? She wanted to do something nice for Paul. She invited him to stay at her house.

When Lydia became God's friend, she probably wanted to know more and more about God. Perhaps that's why she wanted Paul to stay at her house—so she could talk with him more.

The best way to become friends with someone is to spend time with that person and get to know all you can about that person.

MoM'S TOUCH

Tell your daughter about one of your close friends. Why are you and your friend so close? Do you have the same interests or hobbies? Do you have the same kinds of personalities? Has your friend ever done something nice for you? What was it? What kinds of things do you do for your friend?

Ask your daughter to describe her best friend.

Now encourage your daughter in her friendship with God. Discuss how we get to know God and how we stay in touch with him. Encourage her to schedule a time with God every day.

A Verse to Remember

Keep on praying.
1 Thessalonians 5:17

An Angel at the Door

R hoda was a servant girl, so it was a bit of an honor for her to join the Christians' worship service. Tonight was a special prayer service for Peter. Rhoda liked Peter although she was too shy to talk to the loud fisherman. He told wonderful stories that made her laugh.

Peter was in prison. He might even be killed, so the situation was serious. Rhoda found it confusing because Peter's only crime was that he was a Christian.

A soft rumble filled the room as groups of people huddled together, praying for Peter's safety. Rhoda sat in a group near the door. In her heart she prayed as earnestly for Peter as everyone else did, but she was too shy to pray out loud. Sometime late in the evening there was a knock on the door. Rhoda tried to ignore it and concentrate on praying. But the knocking got louder and louder.

Rhoda noticed that the noise was bothering other people, so she went to see who was at the door. When she opened the peek hole, Rhoda couldn't believe who was standing outside. "Rhoda, let me in," Peter said.

Rhoda screamed and ran into the room of praying people. "It's Peter! Peter is at the door!" she shouted.

But no one believed Rhoda. "It can't be Peter. It must be his angel—he must already be dead!" Then the knocking turned to pounding, and all eyes looked at Rhoda. So, once again she went to the door. But this time she remembered to let Peter come in. Every person in the room stood and cheered when Peter walked in.

Peter gave Rhoda a little hug before he began explaining how God had sent an angel to lead him out of the prison. Rhoda listened to Peter's wonderful story of how God had miraculously freed him. Rhoda joined the others as they happily shouted, "Praise God!"

Based on Acts 12:12–17

Becoming a Woman of God
A woman of God serves others

Rhoda was a servant girl. Her job was to do things for other people or help others with the jobs they had to do.

Sometimes people think that a sign of real success in life is to have people who will do your jobs for you—someone to clean your house, do your yardwork, or even drive your car for you. But Jesus showed by the way he lived, and what he taught, that children of God should serve others, not be served.

MOM'S TOUCH

Share with your daughter a time when someone served you by doing something for you without being asked. How did you feel about that person? After that experience, how did you feel about doing things for other people?

Talk with your daughter about how she can share God's love with others by serving them. Talk about ways she can serve other people. Remind her that it's important to have a humble attitude and not demand praise for serving others.

A Verse to Remember

For even I, the Son of Man,
came here not to be served
but to serve others, and to give
my life as a ransom for many.

Matthew 20:28

Part 2

Stories for Fathers and Daughters

Dear Dads,

The relationship a little girl has with her dad is so important. A good relationship helps establish a good self-image and self-confidence. Most little girls think their dads can do absolutely anything. Dad has a unique ability to teach his daughter the truths of the Bible and how to apply Scripture to life.

The *Little Girls Bible Storybook* provides an opportunity to look at well-loved Bible stories through the eyes and hearts of the Bible characters who lived them. We don't really know how these people felt about the experiences they lived through. But they were people like we are, so we can imagine how they felt. By thinking about how these people may have felt, we can learn lessons of how to apply Scripture to our lives and how to make God real in every aspect of life.

Caron Turk has once again hidden a little angel in each illustration. I know that you and your little girl will have fun looking for this little angel. Hopefully, you'll be able to discuss the Bible story as you do your angel search. Caron and I pray that this book will provide hours of "together time" and entertainment with a purpose for you and your daughter. We pray that you will grow closer together and that both you and your daughter will go deeper in your relationship with the Lord through reading and talking about this book.

God bless,

Carolyn Larsen

Someone Like Me

Plink, plink, plink, splash! Adam absentmindedly skipped rocks across a lake filled with water so blue that it almost hurt his eyes. He didn't even seem to notice the animals playing around him. Tiring of the rock-skipping game, Adam leaned back against a tree and heaved a big sigh.

"What's the matter, Son? You don't seem very happy," the Father asked gently.

"I'm sorry, Father. I don't know what's wrong. Maybe I'm a little, ummmmm, lonely." Adam didn't mean to be disrespectful. After all, God had given him a beautiful garden to live in and lots of different kinds of animals to play with.

"I know what's wrong," the Father said, still very gently. "You need someone to talk to—someone who is more like you than any of the animals are."

"Yeah! I think you're right." Adam jumped to his feet in excitement. "But, there isn't anyone here like me. So what do we do?"

"Why don't you take a nap while I work on this?" God seemed to be smiling as he spoke.

Carefully, so as not to disturb Adam's sleep, God gently tugged a rib from Adam's side and used it to make a new person. She was sort of like Adam, but not exactly. "Welcome to earth, Eve. You will be Adam's wife." God was extra gentle now. Eve looked around at the beautiful flowers and rivers. She saw soft bunnies and fuzzy squirrels playing in the grass. She knew that she would be very happy here.

"Adam, wake up," God whispered. Adam opened his eyes and saw a woman with long, curly hair. She smiled shyly at him. "This is Eve," God said. "She will be your wife. I know you will be very happy together. I made you both to be a lot like me. You can think and talk and laugh and cry. I'd like you to take care of things here in the garden."

Adam took Eve's hand. It felt nice. Adam knew that he wouldn't ever be lonely again.

Based on Genesis 1–2

Becoming a Woman of God

A Woman of God is made in God's image

God made people in his image. That means we are a lot like him. It's important for us to remember that all people are made in God's image. When we remember this, we will treat other people with kindness and respect.

It's also important to remember that God made you to be exactly the way he wants you to be. So, be happy with who you are and be thankful for the things you can do!

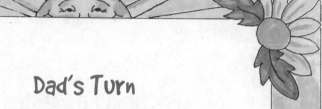

Dad's Turn

Tell your daughter a story about a skill or ability that God gave you—skill in sports or music, or a love for science or history. Tell her how you have worked to develop that skill or ability.

It's important for your daughter to know how special she is to you. Help her develop a good self-image by pointing out the special things you love about her—her sense of humor, how kind she is, a sports skill, or love for music.

A Verse to Remember

So God created people in his own image;
God patterned them after himself.

Genesis 1:27

Houseboat Safety

Genesis 7-9

"I miss my friends," Noah's wife sighed. "I know God said to build this boat, but . . ."

"I know," Noah interrupted. "If people would just start obeying God again. Then he wouldn't be sending a flood and we wouldn't be building this boat . . . and our friends wouldn't think we're crazy!"

"And, all these animals wouldn't be coming." Mrs. Noah shivered when she saw the snakes and spiders.

Of course, God was right about the flood. As soon as the animals and the Noah family had climbed inside the boat, it started to rain outside. Mrs. Noah missed sunshine and fresh air. But, she kept busy caring for the animals and keeping the boat clean. *It's rained for more than a month*, she thought one night. *The whole earth must be flooded by now*. It made her sad to think that all her friends had drowned. *Why didn't they just listen to God?* she wondered.

One morning when Mrs. Noah woke up she noticed that something was different. "Hmm, what could it be?" Suddenly she knew—"Noah, the rain has stopped!" Just as she said that, the boat bumped something and dishes tumbled from shelves and tables.

"Ground! We've hit ground!" Noah shouted. He peeked out and saw that the boat was sitting on the very tip top of a big mountain. All around them was water.

Day after day Noah checked to see if the flood waters were gone. Finally, one day he called, "I'm opening the door. We can leave the boat!"

"Yahoo!" Mrs. Noah shooed out animals and grabbed a broom. Quickly sweeping the boat clean, she joined Noah on wonderful, dry ground. She grabbed Noah's hand and danced in joy.

The Noah family were the only people left on earth. The first thing they did was thank God for keeping them safe in the great big, sort of smelly, kind of crowded houseboat. Right in the middle of the celebrating, Mrs. Noah noticed colorful arches in the sky. "What is that?" she asked.

"It's a rainbow," God answered. "It's a symbol of my promise to you—I will never send a flood to destroy the whole earth again. So, every time you see a rainbow, remember how very much I love you!"

Based on Genesis 7–9

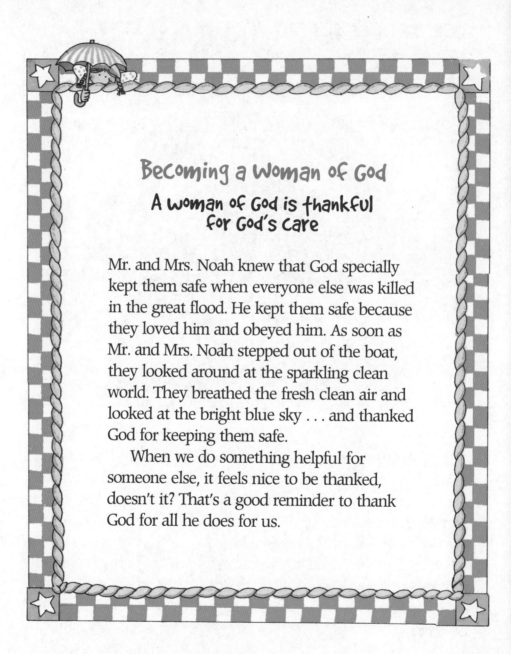

Becoming a Woman of God

A Woman of God is thankful for God's care

Mr. and Mrs. Noah knew that God specially kept them safe when everyone else was killed in the great flood. He kept them safe because they loved him and obeyed him. As soon as Mr. and Mrs. Noah stepped out of the boat, they looked around at the sparkling clean world. They breathed the fresh clean air and looked at the bright blue sky . . . and thanked God for keeping them safe.

When we do something helpful for someone else, it feels nice to be thanked, doesn't it? That's a good reminder to thank God for all he does for us.

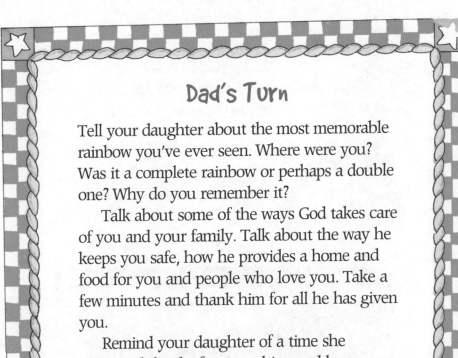

Dad's Turn

Tell your daughter about the most memorable rainbow you've ever seen. Where were you? Was it a complete rainbow or perhaps a double one? Why do you remember it?

Talk about some of the ways God takes care of you and your family. Talk about the way he keeps you safe, how he provides a home and food for you and people who love you. Take a few minutes and thank him for all he has given you.

Remind your daughter of a time she expressed thanks for something and how proud you were of her for doing that.

A Verse to Remember

Give thanks to the LORD, for he is good!

1 Chronicles 16:34

Choosing Your Way
GENESIS 13

Lot sighed and leaned his chair back on two legs. Lot's life was good—he had lots of sheep, cattle, and hundreds of men working for him.

Lot's uncle, Abram, was even richer in gold, silver, sheep, cattle, and people working for him. Both clans had just set up camp near the Jordan River.

"Hey, get your sheep out of here. We got here first!" Lot's shepherds shouted. They poked at Abram's sheep with their staffs, trying to shove them out of the way. Pretty soon the two groups of men were pushing each other and shouting. The sheep didn't know what to think.

Abram sat outside his tent and listened to the arguing. *This isn't right,* he thought. *Someone is going to get hurt if this fighting doesn't stop.* So, he went to see his nephew. "We've got to stop fighting. Look, we've got all this land around us. Why don't we go our separate ways? Then there will be plenty of food and water for our animals."

"You're right," Lot agreed. He looked around at the wide open countryside. The land around the Jordan River looked like a garden. There would be plenty of food there for his animals. He knew that the land farther away was more like a desert. It would be harder to find food and water there.

"I'll stay here," Lot announced. Abram didn't say a word. He just packed up his tent and his animals and moved away from the Jordan River. "Abram," God whispered, "look around you. I'm going to give all this land to you someday. You will have as many children as there are stars in the sky. I'm going to bless you, Abram."

Based on Genesis 13

Becoming a Woman of God
A Woman of God seeks peace

Abram could have argued with Lot because he wanted the best land. After all, he was older and Lot should have let him have first choice of where to live. But, Abram didn't fight with Lot. It was more important to him to have peace with his nephew. It was a better example of God's love. He knew that God would take care of him, wherever he was.

How good are you at living peacefully with other people? Do you ever argue with your brothers or sisters? Do you fight with your friends? Do you always want to have your own way? What do you learn from Abram about this kind of behavior?

Dad's Turn

Talk about how you got along with your siblings or friends when you were a child. Did you have a brother or a friend with whom you were very competitive? How did that affect your relationship?

Talk to your daughter about how she relates to others. Recall a time when she went out of her way to be peaceful with someone who was being selfish. Congratulate her on her behavior. Talk about what situations make her angry or impatient. Talk about how to handle those feelings.

A Verse to Remember

Live in harmony and peace.

2 Corinthians 13:11

Genesis 26:18-25 ♥

"My daddy built this well. The Philistines closed it after he died and I think it's time to reopen it," Isaac announced. His servants worked hard to dig out the dirt that plugged up the well.

"Yahoo! Water for us and our herds!" Isaac's workers cheered. But their happiness didn't last long. Men who worked for Gerar ran up shouting, "This is our land, so this well you just dug belongs to us."

"Fight for our well," Isaac's men shouted. But, Isaac didn't want to fight. He took his men and his herds and moved to a new place.

"Dig another well here," he told his men. Once again the men dug a well and cheered when they had fresh water. But again, Gerar's men came and claimed the well.

Isaac and his men moved again and dug a third well.
"I hope he doesn't let those creeps take this well, too,"
Isaac's men grumbled. They wanted to celebrate the
fresh cool water, but they were afraid to be too happy.

Isaac studied the horizon, watching for Gerar's men to come and argue about this well, too. One day passed, then two—no one came. Finally, Isaac felt that it was safe to celebrate. "This is where God wants us to stay," he announced.

While Isaac's men tossed water in the air, shouting and celebrating, Isaac thanked God. "I will bless you, Isaac," God promised. "You will have more descendants than you can even imagine!"

Based on Genesis 26:18–25

Becoming a Woman of God
A Woman of God Chooses her battles

Isaac was the son of Abraham, a great man of God. All his life Isaac had watched how Abraham lived his life. He saw him stand up and hold his ground when he needed to and he probably saw him sometimes turn and walk away from a fight. He saw that Abraham loved God and lived for him every day. A child learns a lot by watching how his dad lives.

Even though Isaac's workers pushed him to fight for their wells, Isaac knew that wasn't the right thing to do. This wasn't the right time to fight. At some time in life, everybody faces a bully who tries to take what's not theirs. Isaac knew how to handle this instance.

Dad's Turn

Can you share an example of a time when you resisted the urge to fight for something? Were you later glad that you did? How did the problem get solved? Did you talk it through with the other person, or just walk away?

Tell your daughter about a time when you did stand firm and fight for something you believed in or something you owned. Talk to your daughter about bullies she may meet someday who will try to push her around or take her things. Help her plan out gentle (but firm) ways to handle these situations. Help her understand that fighting isn't always the best (or safest) way to handle problems.

A Verse to Remember

The LORD is my strength and my song; he has become my victory.

Exodus 15:2

Grapeland

Numbers 13-14

"Last, but not least, I choose Caleb and Joshua. You twelve men will sneak into the land of Canaan," Moses announced. "God wants you to check out the land. Is the soil good? Do good crops grow there? Do the towns have walls? Are the armies big?" Moses gave instructions to the men who were running around trying to get organized.

One afternoon the spies were carefully picking their way down the side of a mountain. "Careful, don't slip!" someone called. When all twelve were safely down the men took a minute to look around.

"Look at the size of those grapes!" one man whispered. "I've never seen anything like this. Let's cut a cluster and take it back to show everyone."

Forty days after leaving on their special mission, the twelve men returned to Moses and reported. "Wonderful crops grow in Canaan—just look at these huge grapes. It's a beautiful land, with lots of space for us and plenty of food and water."

"Yeah, but on the other hand, the people there are giants . . . I mean GIANTS! And the cities have big walls around them," another man said.

The spies argued among themselves about whether or not the Israelites should try to capture the land. Two spies—Joshua and Caleb—said, "Let's go for it. God already said that the land is ours!" But, the other ten were chicken because of the giants.

The people listened to the spies argue and finally someone said, "I agree with the ten—there's no way we could capture Canaan." The whole crowd sided with the ten who were chicken. Caleb and Joshua were very frustrated.

God was even more frustrated than Caleb and Joshua. "I told you that I was giving you the land. Since you don't believe me–you will wander around for forty years (one year for every day the spies were gone). After that I'll give you this land–but none of you will be alive to see it–except Caleb and Joshua, who believed me."

Based on Numbers 13–14

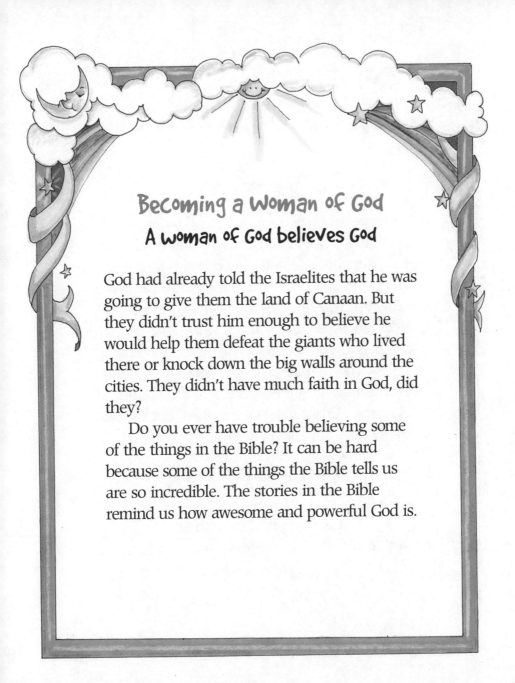

Becoming a Woman of God
A Woman of God believes God

God had already told the Israelites that he was going to give them the land of Canaan. But they didn't trust him enough to believe he would help them defeat the giants who lived there or knock down the big walls around the cities. They didn't have much faith in God, did they?

Do you ever have trouble believing some of the things in the Bible? It can be hard because some of the things the Bible tells us are so incredible. The stories in the Bible remind us how awesome and powerful God is.

Dad's Turn

Do you easily believe new things? Or are you from Missouri—the "SHOW ME" state? Tell your daughter about something you once found it difficult to believe. Perhaps the whole concept of heaven was difficult to grasp. Or maybe there are other things in our world that are so amazing to you that they are difficult to believe.

Ask your daughter if there is anything that she has trouble understanding and therefore believing. Perhaps you can explain that thing so simply that she understands it.

A Verse to Remember

What is faith?
It is the confident assurance
that what we hope for is going to happen.
Hebrews 11:1

Showdown at the Old Oak Tree

Judges 6:1-24

"God, save us!" the Israelite people prayed day after day. They sort of forgot that the reason they were having so many problems was because they kept disobeying God. "Our enemies are so mean that we have to hide in the mountains. We've lost our homes, our cattle, our crops. God, we're starving!"

God heard their cries and sent an angel to sit beneath an old oak tree where Gideon was secretly threshing wheat. He was going to hide it from their enemies. "Right here, the Lord is with you!" the angel said.

"Oh right," Gideon snapped. "If God is with us, then why are we having so many problems?"

"God is sending you to rescue the people," the angel answered.

"Gulp!" Gideon didn't know what to think about that. "Whoa, that can't be—I'm a nobody—surely I'm not the best choice. I'm going to need some proof that God really wants me for this job."

The angel waited patiently while Gideon hurried home to cook a goat and bake some bread. When he returned, the angel said, "Put it on that rock over there and pour broth over it."

"Stand back!" the angel shouted. He touched the dripping meat and bread with his staff and fire shot out from the rock. Every drop of meat, bread, and gravy burned right up. Now Gideon knew that God wanted him to do this job.

Based on Judges 6:1–24

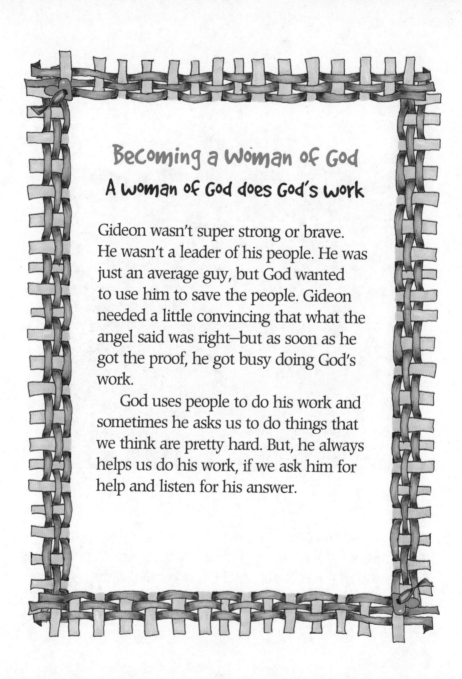

Becoming a Woman of God
A Woman of God does God's Work

Gideon wasn't super strong or brave. He wasn't a leader of his people. He was just an average guy, but God wanted to use him to save the people. Gideon needed a little convincing that what the angel said was right—but as soon as he got the proof, he got busy doing God's work.

God uses people to do his work and sometimes he asks us to do things that we think are pretty hard. But, he always helps us do his work, if we ask him for help and listen for his answer.

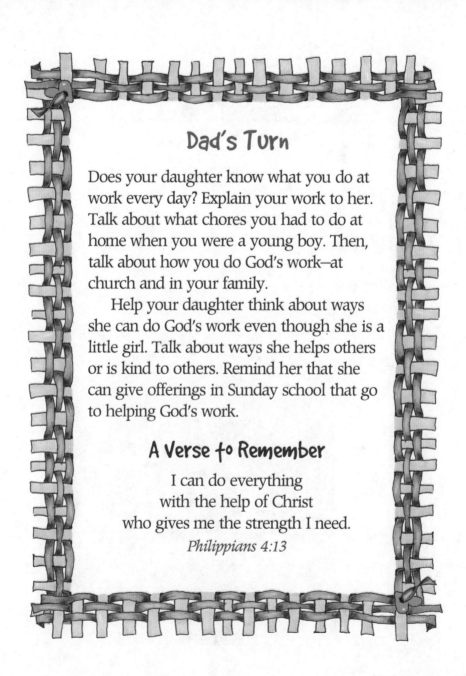

Dad's Turn

Does your daughter know what you do at work every day? Explain your work to her. Talk about what chores you had to do at home when you were a young boy. Then, talk about how you do God's work—at church and in your family.

Help your daughter think about ways she can do God's work even though she is a little girl. Talk about ways she helps others or is kind to others. Remind her that she can give offerings in Sunday school that go to helping God's work.

A Verse to Remember

I can do everything
with the help of Christ
who gives me the strength I need.

Philippians 4:13

Nighttime ☆ Obedience

JUDGES 6:25-32

"Gideon, I'm tired of Israel worshipping other gods. Help me put a stop to it—tear down your dad's altar to Baal and cut down the Asherah pole that's next to it. Build an altar to me in its place," God said.

"Everyone in town worships Baal. If I knock down their altar, they're going to be really mad." Gideon was a little nervous.

But God didn't change his request. So, Gideon waited until it was dark and everyone was sleeping. He ordered his servants, "Pull down this altar, stone by stone. Don't leave one stone in place." While they worked on that, Gideon cut down the Asherah pole. But, the whole time he kept looking around to make sure no one was coming.

When the altar was down, Gideon built an altar to
God. Heaving a big bull onto it, he sacrificed it to God.
"Father, thank you for loving us. Forgive your people
once again for turning away from you." As the sun
peeked over the horizon, Gideon tumbled into bed.

Father, forgive your people again for turning away from you

Father, thank you for forgiving us

It didn't take long the next morning for people to notice what had happened. "Hey, what happened to Baal's altar?" "Yeah, and to the Asherah pole? Who would do this?"

"Someone built a new altar and sacrificed a bull to God." Quickly a mob started looking for the person who had done this. The evidence pointed to Gideon.

"Give us your son. He's going to pay for this!" the mob shouted at Joash. "He wrecked Baal's altar!" Gideon hid behind a door and prayed.

His dad looked around at his friends and neighbors before saying, "Why are you fighting Baal's battle? If he's really so powerful, let him rebuild his altar and take care of my son. Maybe we should be worshipping the real God instead of a fake one."

Based on Judges 6:25–32

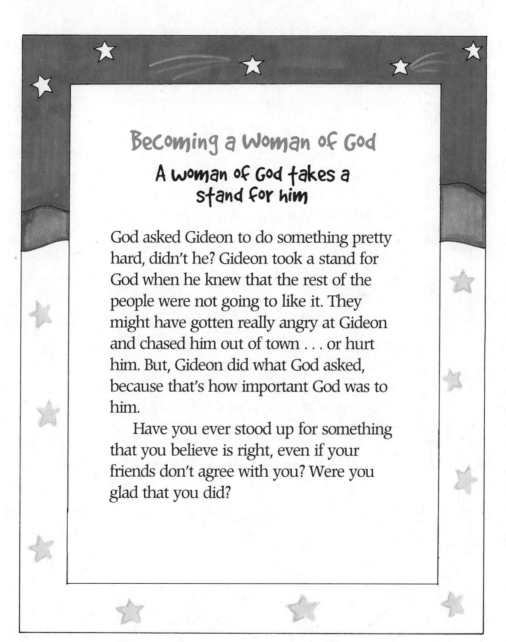

Becoming a Woman of God
A woman of God takes a stand for him

God asked Gideon to do something pretty hard, didn't he? Gideon took a stand for God when he knew that the rest of the people were not going to like it. They might have gotten really angry at Gideon and chased him out of town . . . or hurt him. But, Gideon did what God asked, because that's how important God was to him.

Have you ever stood up for something that you believe is right, even if your friends don't agree with you? Were you glad that you did?

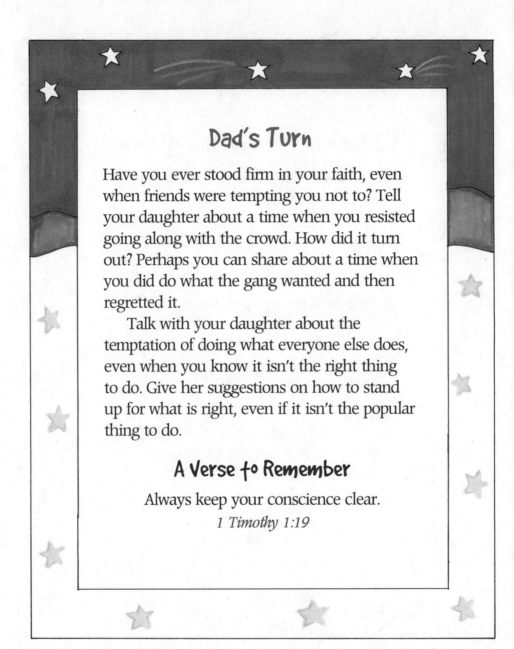

Dad's Turn

Have you ever stood firm in your faith, even when friends were tempting you not to? Tell your daughter about a time when you resisted going along with the crowd. How did it turn out? Perhaps you can share about a time when you did do what the gang wanted and then regretted it.

Talk with your daughter about the temptation of doing what everyone else does, even when you know it isn't the right thing to do. Give her suggestions on how to stand up for what is right, even if it isn't the popular thing to do.

A Verse to Remember

Always keep your conscience clear.
1 Timothy 1:19

You're the ♥ One!

1 SAMUEL 16:1-13

"Naa naa naa na naa ya, we're going to meet Samuel the priest and you're not!" David's older brother loved to tease him. "You're just a baby—only good for taking care of the sheep. We OLDER brothers have more important things to do."

"He's only a little bit older than me," David thought. "I wish I
could go to the meeting with Samuel." He turned around to see
his father and all seven of his older brothers leaving for town
and the meeting with Samuel and all the town leaders. Dragging
his staff in the dirt, David headed for the field.

David settled down near his sheep and
began playing his harp. It was peaceful
and quiet on the hillside. Meanwhile at the
meeting in town, Samuel asked to meet David's
older brothers. Eliab, the oldest, came to Samuel. He was
tall and strong and very handsome. Samuel seemed excited
to meet him, but after a few minutes of silence, he asked to
meet the next boy.

Soon Samuel had met all of the boys. He seemed to be looking for something or someone . . . but he didn't find it with any of them. Turning to Jesse, he asked, "Do you have any other sons?"

"Well, my youngest is at home watching the sheep. But, he's just a little tyke; why would you care about him?" Jesse answered.

All Samuel would say was, "Go get him."

As soon as David came into the room, Samuel ran to him and laid his hands on David's small shoulders. "You're the one," he whispered. "God has told me that you will be king of Israel. I am here to anoint you." David was filled with joy as Samuel poured the anointing oil on his head. God hadn't chosen any of his older, taller, stronger, handsomer brothers—God chose David.

Based on 1 Samuel 16:1–13

Becoming a Woman of God
A Woman of God may be a Child

David's older brother wasn't too nice, was he? He thought that David wasn't worth much because he was just a little guy. But, God doesn't look at how big or strong we are. He doesn't care if we're pretty or handsome. God looks at our hearts. He looks to see if we love him and want to serve him. He looks to see if we care about other people. Even a child can have a heart that loves God.

Dad's Turn

When did you come to faith in God? Were you a young person or an adult? If you were a child, tell your daughter about the experience. Tell her ways you got involved in God's work as a young person.

Help your daughter see ways that she can serve God as a young person. Plan a family time of serving at an inner city ministry or food pantry. Show her the practical ways of helping others and serving God.

A Verse to Remember

Don't let anyone think less of you because you are young. Be an example to all believers in what you teach, in the way you live, in your love, your faith, and your purity.

1 Timothy 4:12

A STONE'S THROW

"**Y**ou're always acting like such a big shot. Why don't you just go home?" Eliab shoved his little brother and David tumbled to the ground.

"Father sent me here to bring this stuff to you guys," David tried to explain. "I was just looking around. I've never seen an army camp before."

"How come none of King Saul's soldiers will fight that Philistine giant, Goliath?" he continued. But Eliab didn't answer, he just stomped away.

Just then David heard Goliath shouting again, "Hey, you Israelite chickens. Send someone out to fight me! Come on, don't you think your big, powerful God will help you?"

"Ooooo, that creep. How can you guys let him make fun of God like that?" David looked around at the big, strong soldiers. None of them would even look back at him. So, David marched into King Saul's tent and shouted, "I'm just a kid, but I'll fight the giant. Just let me at him!"

King Saul looked at shrimpy little David, then he looked out at the giant Goliath . . . "OK, but at least wear my armor!" he said. But, when David got it on, he couldn't move. "Hey, I can't walk . . . I can't even see . . . this stuff is too heavy. Take it off! I'm going to do this my way!" he shouted.

Hurrying down the hill, David stopped to pick up 5 stones. When Goliath saw that a kid was coming to fight him, he got boiling mad! He shouted and stomped and sputtered. *Give it up, Big Guy; you can't win because God is helping me*, David thought. He calmly put a stone in his slingshot and swung it around and around. The stone flew through the air and THWACKED into Goliath's head. The earth shook as the giant dropped to the ground. "David won! David won!" King Saul's soldiers shouted.

Based on 1 Samuel 17:1–51

Becoming a Woman of God

A Woman of God stands in God's strength

David knew that he wasn't fighting alone. He knew that a little kid like him wouldn't have a chance against a nine-foot-tall giant soldier like Goliath—except that God was helping him. That was something that King Saul's soldiers didn't understand, or one of them would have fought the giant.

When you have Christ living in your heart, you are never alone. He will help you with the tough things you may have to do, if you just ask him.

Dad's Turn

Recall a time when you had to do something that really scared you. Maybe it was public speaking, maybe it was moving to a new state—whatever it was, it was not easy! Tell your daughter about it. Tell her why it was scary to you and tell her how you got through it.

Ask your daughter what kinds of things she thinks are frightening. Talk about how to handle those things. Pray together for God's strength to help her do hard things.

A Verse to Remember

For nothing is impossible with God.

Luke 1:37

Now Showing A "Command Performance"

BASED ON 2 SAMUEL 9

"Are you Mephibosheth?" a mean-looking soldier growled. For just a minute Mephibosheth thought about saying, "No." After all, why would one of King David's soldiers be looking for him? "Well?" the soldier asked. Mephibosheth knew that this guy wasn't going away so he finally admitted that he was.

"Come with me. King David wants to see you," the soldier said as he turned away.

Well, this can't be good. Why would King David want to see me? My grandpa, King Saul, tried for years to kill King David. So, what if the king is going to put me in jail—or do something worse—because of what my grandfather did? he wondered.

Mephibosheth followed behind the soldier as quickly as he could. His feet were crippled from a childhood accident so walking was not easy. The soldier led him right to King David. Mephibosheth dropped to his knees. He had never been this close to the famous king. His heart was pounding so hard that he thought the king must be able to hear it.

King David gently lifted Mephibosheth to his feet. "Your father, Jonathan, was the best friend I've ever had," the king said. "I promised him a long time ago that when I became king I would take care of his children and grandchildren. You're the only one who is still alive. I want to keep my promise to Jonathan." Mephibosheth didn't know what to say, so he just stood there staring at the great king.

"I'd like you to come live here in the palace with me." Mephibosheth looked around at the grand palace. He had never seen anything so beautiful. "You can eat all your meals with me. I will give back to you all the land that once belonged to your grandfather, and I will have someone farm it to grow food for your family." Mephibosheth was amazed at King David's kindness. He bowed to the king, thanking him over and over.

Based on 2 Samuel 9

Becoming a Woman of God
A Woman of God is kind

King David didn't have to be kind to
Mephibosheth. No one knew about his
promise to Jonathan, except him and God.
But, King David loved God and tried to live
for him. Keeping the promise he had made
was one way to show others that God was
important to him.

Do you take your promises seriously?
Or do you promise, "I'll clean my room after
lunch," and then forget about it completely?
If you keep your promises, it shows you
have an honest heart and that how you
treat others is important to you.

Dad's Turn

Have you ever made a promise without really thinking about how difficult it would be to keep it? Did you keep it anyway? Tell your daughter about a time when you kept a promise, even though it wasn't easy for you. Tell her how you felt afterwards.

Help your daughter understand that something as simple as keeping a promise can show others how important God is to us. It's a way of witnessing that God lives in our hearts. Remind her to think before she makes a promise and not to make a promise that she can't keep.

A Verse to Remember

Don't lie to each other.

Colossians 3:9

BIRD FEEDER

Ahab was the worst king Israel had ever, ever had. He didn't care a bit about God or any of God's rules for living. He was mean and selfish and cheated people. To make things even worse, he married Jezebel, who worshipped fake gods—so he did, too. Ahab made God more angry than any other king before him. God decided to get Ahab's attention.

"Elijah, tell Ahab that it isn't going to rain in Israel for years until you say so—because I say so!"

"Ahab isn't going to be happy about this!" Elijah was a little worried.

"Don't worry about him," God said. "Go hide in the forest by the Kerith Brook. I'll take care of you."

Elijah gave Ahab the God-is-mad-so-it's-not-going-to-rain-for-a-long-time news. Then he ran for his life. He set up camp by Kerith Brook. And waited. Hot sunshine quickly dried up ponds and rivers all around Israel. Elijah knew that people were going hungry and thirsty because there was no rain to make the food grow and no water to drink.

Slurping a drink of cool, clear water from Kerith Brook, Elijah wondered what he was going to do when his food ran out. One morning Elijah woke up to a strange sound. He peeked open an eye to see a big raven nearby with a hunk of bread in its beak. "Yahoo! Food! God is sending me food!" Elijah shouted.

The next morning Elijah woke up wondering if the raven would come back. Sure enough, every morning and every night the raven brought meat and bread for him. So, Elijah stayed hidden by the Kerith Brook, until all of its water dried up, too. Then God sent him somewhere else.

Based on 1 Kings 17:1–7

Becoming a Woman of God
A Woman of God is Cared for by God

God never leaves us to stumble through life by ourselves. He knew that King Ahab was going to be plenty angry at Elijah and even blame Elijah because it didn't rain. So, God took care of Elijah. He sent him to a safe place and provided food and water for him.

It's hard to not worry about things that happen to us . . . or that we are afraid may happen to us. But, stories like this one remind us that God will always take care of us; all we have to do is trust him.

Dad's Turn

When was a time that you worried about something? Maybe there wasn't enough money to pay the bills, or perhaps you lost your job. Did you trust God to meet that need? Have you ever seen God miraculously provide for you? Tell your daughter about it.

Remind your daughter that worrying doesn't help anything . . . it just makes us worry more. Talk about the story of God caring for Elijah and how it can encourage her to trust God to take care of her, too.

A Verse to Remember

Trust in the LORD with all your heart;
do not depend on your own understanding.

Proverbs 3:5

"Shhhh! Did you hear something?"

← CAVE

King Ahab and Queen Jezebel were hopping mad! From their viewpoint being mad made perfect sense; after all, Elijah had killed 400 prophets of the fake god, Baal–the god they worshipped. It sure didn't make them look too good. *I better get out of here*, Elijah thought and he headed for the hills . . . actually Mt. Sinai.

Elijah ran and ran, finally collapsing inside a cave tucked away near the top of the mountain. "What are you doing here?" a voice rang through the darkness.

Elijah knew it was God's voice. "Look, I've spent my life teaching Israel about you. But, the people break their promises to you, tear down your altars, even kill your prophets—I'm the only one left! I can't take it anymore; I'm hiding here!"

"Go outside. Stand on the mountain," God commanded. Elijah crept just outside the cave opening and looked up at the sky. Suddenly a ferocious wind began to blow. It blew harder and harder until rocks pulled away from the mountain and tumbled down. Elijah held on for dear life. "God," he said, "was I supposed to hear your voice in this powerful wind?"

The earth began to shake and roll as if someone had picked up the mountain and was shaking it as hard as they could. Elijah fell to his knees and held on to a tree trunk. *Is God trying to speak to me now?* he wondered.

Then he heard a hissing sound and looked up to see a wall of fire roaring up the mountain. Dashing back into the cave, Elijah listened for God to speak . . . but he heard nothing.

Hang on Elijah!

When the fire passed, Elijah stood up and brushed himself off—this had been quite a day. That's when he heard it . . . a gentle whisper floating up the mountain . . . the voice of God: "You aren't really alone, Elijah. There are still others who love me. Just keep on doing my work."

Based on 1 Kings 19:8–18

Becoming a Woman of God
A Woman of God listens for his Voice

Have you ever noticed how noisy our
world is? We learn from Elijah that we
should get away from the noise and
busyness of our world in order to hear
God's voice. He won't try to compete with
television noise or noisy playmates. To
hear God's voice we need to be in a quiet
place for awhile . . . and listen. When God
speaks to us, it probably won't be in a
voice that sounds like a person; it's more
like a whisper inside your heart.

Do you sometimes spend quiet time
just listening to the world around you? Do
you ever hear God's voice speaking inside
your heart?

Dad's Turn

How good are you at being quiet? Do you tend to have the TV or radio on as background noise most of the time? Do an experiment with your daughter. Go outside and sit quietly in the park or your backyard. Don't speak at all, just listen for about 10 minutes. Then talk about the sounds that you heard. Did you hear things that you don't usually notice?

Help your daughter establish a quiet time with God every day. Spend 5 or 10 minutes with her. Pray and read a verse of Scripture, then just be quiet for a few minutes.

A Verse to Remember

You should be known for the beauty that comes from within, the unfading beauty of a gentle and quiet spirit, which is precious to God.

1 Peter 3:4

"Momma, why is that man so mean? He scares me." The little boy grabbed his mom's leg and buried his face in her skirt. His older brother tried to act tougher, but fear shone from his eyes, too. Their mom hugged the boys to her side and watched the man walk away. "My boys are right," she thought; "that man is mean."

Of course, she would never say that out loud. She was a gentle woman who tried to raise her sons to be good men. But, ever since her husband died, the mean man had been threatening her. He said her husband had owed him lots of money and he wanted it . . . NOW! The woman looked around her house—she had sold lots of her furniture, and she still didn't have money to pay the man.

Leaving her sons with a neighbor, the woman hurried across town to see Elisha. *If the prophet of God can't help me, no one can*, she thought. Elisha listened as she blurted out her story. He could hear the fear and pain in her voice. "My boys are all I have left. Please don't let him take them," she begged.

Have faith ♥ Elisha will help!

Elisha and the woman hurried to her house. "You have one jar of olive oil here, right?" he asked. She nodded, but thought that was an odd thing to focus on. "Find as many empty jars as you can. Send your sons to borrow some from your neighbors," he ordered. The boys thought this was a great adventure as they hurried from neighbor to neighbor.

"Pour oil into that first jar. Keep filling jars until your own oil jar is empty," Elisha said quietly. The woman didn't even question this odd command. She started pouring oil.

"Boys, bring more jars!" she cried as she filled jar after jar from her one little jar. "Pay attention, sons, you're seeing God take care of us!"

Elisha smiled as he told the woman, "Sell this extra oil. Pay the man and keep whatever money is left over to buy food for your family."

Based on 2 Kings 4:1–7

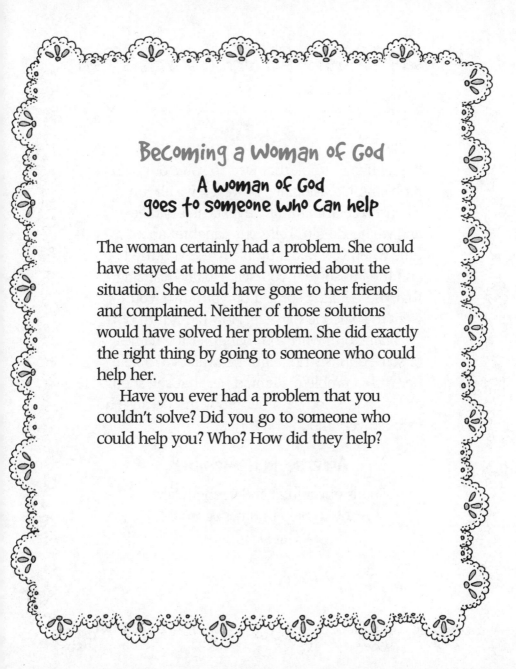

Becoming a Woman of God

A woman of God goes to someone who can help

The woman certainly had a problem. She could have stayed at home and worried about the situation. She could have gone to her friends and complained. Neither of those solutions would have solved her problem. She did exactly the right thing by going to someone who could help her.

Have you ever had a problem that you couldn't solve? Did you go to someone who could help you? Who? How did they help?

Dad's Turn

We all like to think that we can solve our own problems. Occasionally, however, we all run up against something that we just can't handle—and we need help. Tell your daughter about a time when you had a problem and you tried and tried to solve it yourself. Finally, realizing that you couldn't solve it on your own, you went to someone for help. How did it turn out?

Brainstorm with your daughter the names of some adults who might be available to help her with a problem. Remind her that she should always go to God with her problems, because he cares so very much about her.

A Verse to Remember

God is our refuge and strength, always
ready to help in times of trouble.

Psalm 46:1

The Birth of the King

Luke 2:1-20

With every bouncing step the donkey took, Mary wanted to break down and cry. She was tired, every bone in her body hurt, and the baby in her tummy was wiggling his complaints about the long donkey ride. *If only we didn't have to go to Bethlehem to be counted in the census,* she thought.

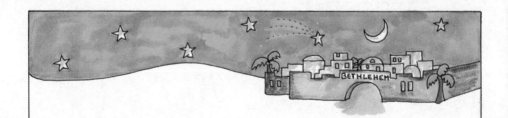

Joseph could have gone alone, but since the baby was due any day Mary didn't want to be away from him. "Are you OK, Mary?" Joseph asked.

She sat up straighter and answered, "Yes, but is it much farther?" She didn't want to worry him, but Mary didn't know how much longer she could ride on this donkey.

"We'll be there soon and we'll get a room with a soft bed so you can rest," Joseph promised.

When they got to Bethlehem, Mary was surprised at the crowded streets. Hundreds of people had come to be counted in the census. She waited while Joseph went to get a room. People pushed past her and animals bellowed. Mary couldn't wait to get inside.

"There aren't any rooms—the whole town is full! The innkeeper said that since you're pregnant, we can stay in his stable. I'm so sorry, but I think it's the best we can do," Joseph apologized.

"It's OK. I just want to lie down," Mary sighed. Sliding from the donkey, she settled down on some clean straw and fell right to sleep. A few hours later a sharp pain shooting through her tummy woke her up. "Joseph . . . the baby. WAKE UP!"

Joseph tried his best to make her comfortable and help in whatever way he could. When he finally laid the newborn baby in her arms, Mary smiled up at him.

Mary wrapped Jesus in a clean blanket and kissed his soft brown hair and pudgy neck. Mary and Joseph sat together and watched in amazement as the new baby slept. "He's the Son of God," Mary whispered. "The Son of God."

"I know," Joseph whispered back. "God is trusting us to raise his Son. This little boy will grow up to be our Savior."

Based on Luke 2:1–20

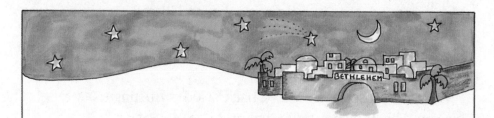

Becoming a Woman of God
A Woman of God knows her Savior

Mary knew Jesus in a way that no one else ever has. She was his earthly mother, but she knew that Jesus would be her Savior, too. Mary was chosen to be Jesus' mother because her heart was so in tune with God. That helped her believe that Jesus wasn't just an ordinary baby.

Do you believe that Jesus is your Savior? Do you understand that you are a sinner and that Jesus died for your sins so you can live in heaven with him someday?

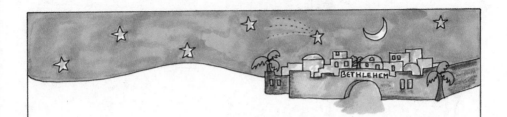

Dad's Turn

Tell your daughter the story of your own salvation. Who led you to the Lord? How did you come to the point of realizing your need for Christ?

Talk to your daughter about her position before God. Has she made a confession of faith? Is she close to understanding how important the birth we celebrate at Christmas is to her?

A Verse to Remember

My sheep recognize my voice;
I know them, and they follow me.
I give them eternal life,
and they will never perish.

John 10:27–28

393

Night Run to Egypt

Matthew 2:1-23

Whew! I'm tired. Bed is going to feel good tonight, Joseph thought. He punched his pillow into a comfortable position and drifted off to sleep. But, just a few hours later something very strange happened. "Joseph, wake up. I have a message for you. It's from God." The voice interrupted Joseph's sleep, just enough for him to peek open one eye; something brilliant white stood in front of him—an angel ... and it looked kind of familiar.

"I know you. You came to me when I was sleeping once before and told me that Mary was going to have a baby that was the Son of God," Joseph whispered, so he wouldn't wake Mary.

"That's right. I am an angel, sent by God. He wants you to get up right now. Take Mary and little Jesus and get out of town," the angel said.

"But why? We're settled here in Bethlehem. I've got a good carpentry business built up and Mary has made friends." Joseph was confused by the command to leave town.

"King Herod wants to kill Jesus—he is jealous that Jesus is called the King of the Jews. You've got to run . . . now. Take your little family and go to Egypt. I'll tell you when it's safe to come home," the angel said firmly. Then he disappeared.

Joseph jumped up and threw a few things into a bag. "Mary, get up. Get Jesus—we've got to get out of town—fast!" Mary knew better than to argue with Joseph when he used that tone of voice. She didn't even take time to pack a few things. As they disappeared into the darkness, Joseph explained what the angel had told him.

The little family arrived safely in Egypt. It was hard to live there
the people spoke a different language and there was no temple
to worship God. "But, Jesus is safe and that's the most important
thing," Joseph reminded Mary when she got discouraged.

A few years later, the angel came again. "It's safe to go home
now. King Herod is dead." Mary and Joseph happily returned to
their hometown, Nazareth. It was good to be with family again!

Based on Matthew 2:1–23

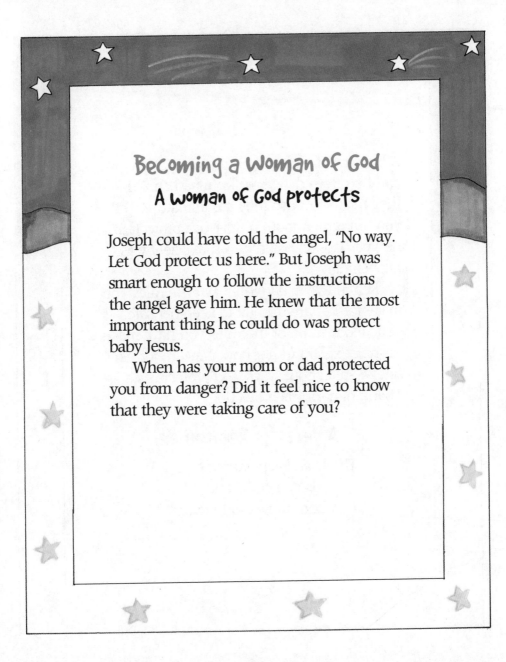

Becoming a Woman of God
A Woman of God protects

Joseph could have told the angel, "No way. Let God protect us here." But Joseph was smart enough to follow the instructions the angel gave him. He knew that the most important thing he could do was protect baby Jesus.

When has your mom or dad protected you from danger? Did it feel nice to know that they were taking care of you?

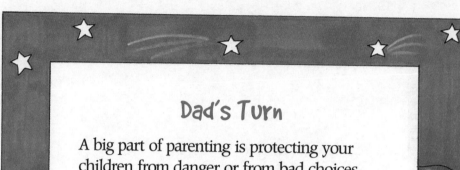

Dad's Turn

A big part of parenting is protecting your children from danger or from bad choices they make because they are immature. Tell your daughter about a time you protected her; perhaps she didn't even realize it was happening.

Remind your daughter that the rules you make for her are usually to keep her safe. Talk about some of the rules you have made for her. Explain to her how they are for her safety. Talk about ways God protects us. Thank him for his protection.

A Verse to Remember

The LORD keeps watch over you
as you come and go,
both now and forever.

Psalm 121:8

The Temptation of Jesus

Jesus was the Son of God. Everyone knew it, at least everyone who was at the Jordan River when John the Baptist baptized Jesus. It was hard to miss because a voice boomed from heaven announcing, "This is my Son and I'm very pleased with him."

Not long after his baptism, Jesus left his mom and dad and everyone he knew. He went out to the wilderness all by himself.

"This is my Son and I'm very pleased with him."

For forty days and forty nights Jesus sat alone in the wilderness.
He had no food and nothing to drink. No friends or family to
talk with . . . the only person who came to be with him was his
biggest enemy . . . Satan.

"What's wrong, Jesus? Are you hungry? Ohhh, poor guy, I can hear your stomach growling. Well, here's an idea—you're the Son of God, right? Why don't you just turn these stones into bread?" Satan snarled, tossing a handful of stones at Jesus' feet.

"No, the Scriptures say that people need more than bread for life. They need to feed on the Word of God," Jesus answered and turned his back on Satan.

Do not test the Lord

Satan whisked Jesus to the highest point at the top of the temple. "If you're really the Son of God, jump off," he challenged. "Your highfalutin Scriptures say that God will send his angels to keep you from so much as stubbing your toe."

"If you really knew the Scriptures you would know they say not to test the Lord," Jesus answered quietly.

Faster than you can say "Hezekiah," Satan took Jesus to the top of a tall mountain. "Look around you—see all the nations of the world? See their glory and riches? Impressive, isn't it? Well, it can all be yours. Yeah, I can give it to you. All you have to do is bow down and worship me." Satan's voice dropped very low.

"Get outta here," Jesus whispered. "The Scriptures say to worship only God!"

Based on Matthew 4:1–11

Becoming a Woman of God
A woman of God fights temptation

Jesus knows what it's like for us when we're tempted to do something wrong. He understands the urge to "take care of number one." He understands the temptation to make yourself more important than others. He understands the pull of being rich and famous. Satan hit him with all those—and Jesus answered each one with a verse of Scripture.

Are you ever tempted to feel more important than someone else or to take the biggest piece of cake? How do you fight temptation?

Dad's Turn

Temptation is a part of life, isn't it? Sometimes Satan is sneaky with temptation and we don't even realize what's happening. Tell your daughter about a temptation you struggle with, for example, the temptation to work too many hours and not be with the family more. Or, temptation to be critical of other people. Tell your daughter how you handle temptation.

Jesus answered Satan with Bible verses. Do you memorize Bible verses? When you are feeling tempted, do those verses ever pop into your mind to help you?

A Verse to Remember

Your word is a lamp for my feet
and a light for my path.

Psalm 119:105

The Beginning

John 2:1-11

Mary didn't get to see Jesus much anymore since he was grown up. He spent most of his time with his friends. So, she was excited to see him at the same wedding celebration she was invited to. The party after the wedding usually lasted for days. Mary enjoyed seeing old friends and catching up with what was happening in their lives.

"Isn't the bride beautiful?" Mary whispered to a friend. The whole event was wonderful, and Mary was happier than she had been in a long time. Then, she heard the master of ceremonies worrying about something. *Oh dear*, she thought. *I hate for anything to spoil this special day. I know Jesus can help.* Searching through the crowd, she saw Jesus and ran to him. "The party isn't over, but they've run out of wine," she told him.

"I can't help them. It's not time for me to do miracles yet," Jesus whispered to her. Mary stared at him with a look that only a mother can give.

Turning to the servants, she said, "Do whatever Jesus tells you to do."

He looked at his mother for a long time, then said, "Fill six big jars with water."

Mary couldn't wait to see what would happen. The servants filled the jars and brought them to Jesus. He didn't even touch them, but just said, "Dip some out and take it to the master of ceremonies."

She wanted to jump up and down in excitement when the man said, "This is the best wine I've ever tasted!" The servants' mouths dropped open—they knew they had put water in those jars—not wine!

Mary looked around for Jesus. She wanted to thank him for helping, but he was nowhere around. Mary knew this was just the first of many miracles he would do. His disciples seemed to be in shock. Now they knew for sure that Jesus wasn't just an ordinary man—he was the Son of God. Mary sighed. "Well, nothing will ever be the same for him now. Soon everyone will know that Jesus is God's own Son."

Based on John 2:1–11

THE WHOLE WORLD WILL KNOW HIM

Becoming a Woman of God

A Woman of God recognizes Jesus' power

Mary knew who Jesus was. She believed in his power and expected him to help people who needed his help. She even expected him to do miracles . . . before he had ever done one. Jesus saw how much faith she had, and he did his first miracle at this wedding. Many more miracles followed.

It's a good thing to see Jesus' power and to expect him to help you when you need it. That's what faith is. Recognizing Jesus' power and expecting him to help you is why you pray to him.

Dad's Turn

Share a story with your daughter of a time when you saw Jesus' power. Perhaps you were made aware of his power through something in nature or through a wonderful answer to prayer.

Did that experience cause you to recognize his power even more and expect answers the next time you prayed?

Encourage your daughter to recognize Jesus' power. Talk about ways you see his power around you. Encourage her to call on that power when she prays and to expect him to answer.

A Verse to Remember

When you ask him, be sure that you really expect him to answer.

James 1:6

Just a Word

Matthew 8:5-13

Polish

"Sir. I polished your shield last night." The servant leaned the shiny shield against the wall and saluted.

The Roman officer had to struggle a bit to keep from patting the servant on the back—that just wasn't something an officer did. "Thank you. I appreciate that you are so attentive. You seem to know what I need before I even know."

The servant bowed slightly as he left the room. He was happy to serve the officer the best way he could. The officer was an important man in the Roman army and he had many servants. Not all of them served happily, so he was especially fond of this good servant—in fact, he almost seemed like a son.

A few days later the officer was working at his desk when another servant dashed into the room. "Forgive me for disturbing you, Sir. But one of your servants is sick—very sick!" The officer ran to the servants' quarters and found his special servant lying in bed, moaning and crying for relief from terrible pain.

The Roman officer didn't know what to do to help his servant. He paced around the room, barking orders for pillows to be brought and ice water. But, he knew he was really helpless. Then he remembered hearing that Jesus was in town. "That's the man who heals sick people using the power of God," he remembered. Grabbing his helmet, he ran for town.

"Sir, my servant is very sick. He's a good servant . . . a good person," the officer told Jesus.

"I'll come and heal him." Jesus was already heading for the officer's house.

"That's not necessary. If you just say the word, I know he will be healed. I have servants; I know that when I speak, they carry out my wishes," the officer said.

Jesus couldn't believe what he was hearing. "I haven't seen this kind of faith ever before," he told his followers. "Go on home," he told the officer. "Your servant is well."

Based on Matthew 8:5–13

Becoming a Woman of God
A woman of God helps others

This Roman officer got quite a compliment from Jesus, didn't he? Jesus said that he had never seen this kind of faith before. The officer didn't think that Jesus had to actually come and touch his servant—he didn't have to come at all. This man had so much faith that he believed Jesus could just say the words and the servant would be healed. The officer wanted to help his servant. He went out of his way to help the sick man.

How big is your faith? When you ask God to do something, do you really truly believe that he will do it? Do you pray for other people and believe that God will answer?

Dad's Turn

The first thing we notice about the Roman officer is that he really cared for his servant–and he sought Jesus' help on his servant's behalf. Tell your daughter about a time when you helped someone else. What did you do? How did you help?

Encourage your daughter to trust God more and more. Help her remember the times that God has answered prayers and met her needs. Help her learn to believe that God can handle anything.

A Verse to Remember

I have trusted in the LORD without wavering.

Psalm 26:1

Getting Out of the BOAT

"Man, I'm tired," Peter announced as he settled down in the boat. Just then the boat lurched sideways and he was nearly tossed out. "Andrew, can't you hold this thing a little steadier?" Peter growled.

"Hey, you're welcome to try it yourself. This storm is getting so bad that the water is bouncing us all over," Andrew shouted back.

"Come on, guys, don't waste energy fighting. We all need to help if we're going to keep ourselves out of the water," John shouted over the sound of the wind. Everyone worked to keep the boat level and keep water out of it.

"I wish Jesus was here," someone said. "Stuff is always okay when he's with us."

"Well, he's not and we're in trouble here!" Peter shouted back. "Get busy!"

For a few minutes all twelve men worked quietly. Then someone said, "Guys, look over there. Do you see something? Is it another boat that's in trouble or what?"

Peter brushed the water from his eyes as he stared through the roaring waves. "It looks more like a man. That's crazy–how could a man be walking around on the water . . . in a storm?"

"It must be a ghost!" Peter suddenly voiced the fear that was in everyone's heart. "God, help us!" he shouted in panic.

"Hey, it's me! Don't be afraid, I'm just coming to help you," a voice called.

"J-J-Jesus???" Peter leaned over the side of the boat to get a better look.  "Jesus, is that you? If it is, let me come to you."

It almost sounded like Jesus was laughing when he called, "Okay, come on!"

In a split second Peter was out of the boat and running across the water! "I'm coming, Jesus!" he called. He looked back at the rest of the disciples in the boat. They were looking at Peter like he had lost his head . . . and when he realized that he was walking on water, Peter sank like a lead weight. "H-e-l-p m-e!!!" he cried.

Jesus was by his side in a minute, lifting him into the boat. As Peter coughed water from his lungs, Jesus quietly said, "You don't have much faith, do you, Peter? Didn't you trust me to keep you safe?"

Based on Matthew 14:22–33

Becoming a Woman of God
A Woman of God gets out of the boat

Peter took a chance—without even thinking about it. He wanted to be with Jesus so badly that he hopped right out of the boat when Jesus called him. Peter would have been OK if he had just kept his eyes on Jesus and not looked back at his buddies. For just an instant, Peter showed awesome faith, the kind of faith that can do exciting things for God.

When have you tried doing something new? Was it exciting or were you afraid? Did you try it a second time, too?

Dad's Turn

Tell your daughter about an experience you had when you tried something new. Was it hard? Were you nervous? Did you enjoy it enough to try it again? Did it change your opinions about things?

Ask your daughter to think about something new she might like to try. Then plan out how you can help her to have a new experience.

A Verse to Remember

The LORD is my light and my salvation,
so why should I be afraid?

Psalm 27:1

The king of a great and powerful land decided to call in all the debts that were owed to him. "Bring the books of my kingdom," he commanded a servant. The king carefully looked through the books to see who owed money to the government. One name jumped out at him—a man who owed him millions of dollars! *My treasury will be even more full if this man pays me back*, the king thought.

"Pay me back now! Otherwise, you, your wife, and your children will be sold as slaves," the king told the man. The poor man was scared silly. His wife and children stood behind him shaking and crying.

"Please, your highness, have mercy on me. I'll pay it all back, I promise. Just give me some time!" he begged. The king had a soft heart, so he released the family—and forgave the debt. The man didn't ever have to pay it back!

The man and his wife danced with joy! "He forgave our debt! We don't have to pay a thing!" They couldn't believe how lucky they were.

As they were walking home, the man saw another man who happened to owe him a few thousand dollars. "Hey you, pay up. I want my money NOW!" He grabbed the man by the collar!

The poor man didn't know what hit him. But, what he did know was that he didn't have any money. "I can't pay—just give me some time and I'll get the money. I promise!"

"Forget it, buddy. You're going to jail!" the angry man shouted. Some of the king's servants saw this whole thing. They knew that the king had forgiven the first man's debt—which was much bigger than the second man's debt.

The servants ran to the king and told him what had happened. He was mad! The king had the first man thrown into jail until he could pay back the millions of dollars he owed the government. "I forgave your big debt. You should have forgiven the other man's debt, too," the king said.

Jesus told this story to teach us about forgiving people because God forgives us.

Based on Matthew 18:23–35

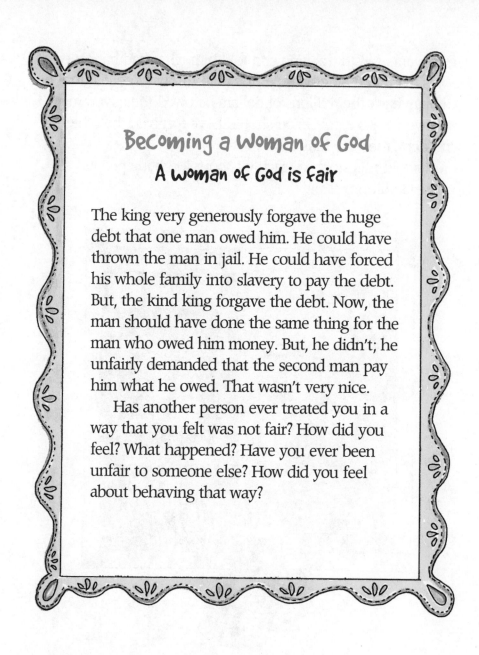

Becoming a Woman of God
A woman of God is fair

The king very generously forgave the huge debt that one man owed him. He could have thrown the man in jail. He could have forced his whole family into slavery to pay the debt. But, the kind king forgave the debt. Now, the man should have done the same thing for the man who owed him money. But, he didn't; he unfairly demanded that the second man pay him what he owed. That wasn't very nice.

Has another person ever treated you in a way that you felt was not fair? How did you feel? What happened? Have you ever been unfair to someone else? How did you feel about behaving that way?

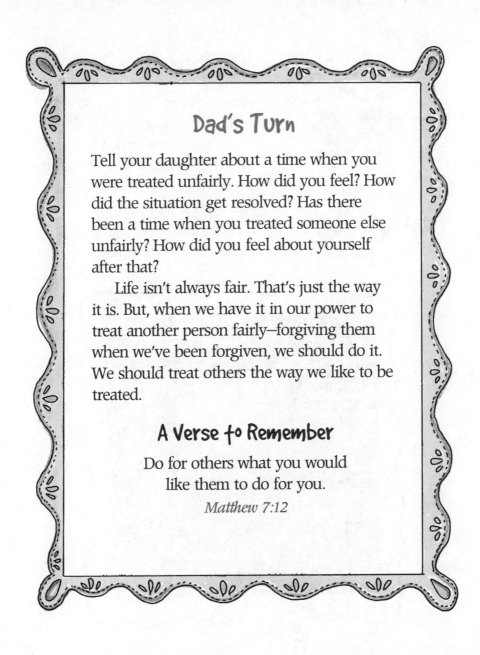

Dad's Turn

Tell your daughter about a time when you were treated unfairly. How did you feel? How did the situation get resolved? Has there been a time when you treated someone else unfairly? How did you feel about yourself after that?

Life isn't always fair. That's just the way it is. But, when we have it in our power to treat another person fairly—forgiving them when we've been forgiven, we should do it. We should treat others the way we like to be treated.

A Verse to Remember

Do for others what you would
like them to do for you.

Matthew 7:12

Following Through

Matthew 21:28-32

"Chores, chores, chores! Why do we have to spend all our time working?" one boy asked, as he finished sweeping the floor.

"Yeah, we're kids. We should be playing games and having fun. There will be plenty of time to work when we're grown up!" his brother answered, putting the last clean plate in the cupboard.

Just then Father came in. "Will you please go pick grapes in the vineyard this afternoon?" he asked his oldest son.

"NO! All I do is work. I'm tired of it." The boy stomped out of the house.

"How about you? Will you help in the vineyards?" Father asked his younger boy.

"I guess so," the boy said. He wasn't excited about it—but he didn't want to argue.

But as he was leaving, the boy's brand new puppy ran up. He started wrestling with the puppy and forgot all about working in the vineyard.

Later, Father came home. "Son, you said you'd pick grapes for me today, but you didn't do it. Since you didn't do what you said you would do, I'm going to have to work overtime to get the work done." Father wasn't very happy.

Father walked slowly to the vineyard. He was tired and disappointed with his son. But, when he got to the vineyard, he saw something that surprised him so much he nearly fainted.

There was his older son working away—picking grapes—the same work he had angrily said he wouldn't do.

"Thank you, thank you, thank you!" Father shouted. "I am so glad you changed your mind. Your brother said he would help, but he didn't. I thought he was the obedient son today—but it really is you because you are actually doing the work!" Father picked up his basket and began working with his son.

Based on Matthew 21:28–32

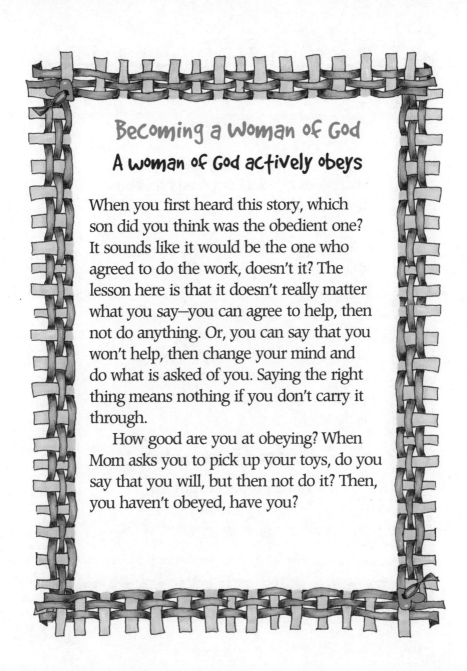

Becoming a Woman of God
A woman of God actively obeys

When you first heard this story, which son did you think was the obedient one? It sounds like it would be the one who agreed to do the work, doesn't it? The lesson here is that it doesn't really matter what you say—you can agree to help, then not do anything. Or, you can say that you won't help, then change your mind and do what is asked of you. Saying the right thing means nothing if you don't carry it through.

How good are you at obeying? When Mom asks you to pick up your toys, do you say that you will, but then not do it? Then, you haven't obeyed, have you?

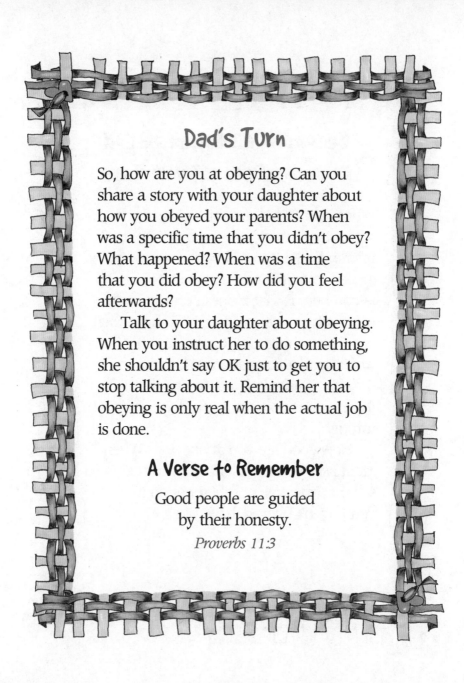

Dad's Turn

So, how are you at obeying? Can you share a story with your daughter about how you obeyed your parents? When was a specific time that you didn't obey? What happened? When was a time that you did obey? How did you feel afterwards?

Talk to your daughter about obeying. When you instruct her to do something, she shouldn't say OK just to get you to stop talking about it. Remind her that obeying is only real when the actual job is done.

A Verse to Remember

Good people are guided
by their honesty.

Proverbs 11:3

A Surprise Friend

BASED ON
LUKE 10:30-37

"Honey, I'm going," a man called as he stuffed a bag of coins into his pocket.

"OK, be careful," his wife answered from the backyard where she was hanging out laundry. The man set out on his weekly walk to Jericho to do business.

He was enjoying his walk, until two men jumped him from behind. They hit him and kicked him until he dropped to the ground. They must have thought he was dead, so they took his money and shoes . . . even his clothes.

"Ohhh," the man moaned. "I hurt all over. Who's going to help me here on this empty road?" He thought for sure he would die there. But, then he heard footsteps. It took all of his energy to lift his head to see who was coming. "Oh, thank the Lord, it's a priest! If anyone will stop to help me, a priest will." But, the priest curled up his nose and said right out loud, "What is this mess doing in my way?" He crossed the road and kept right on walking.

The sun was straight overhead now and the poor man was hot and thirsty. "Maybe I'm dreaming, but I think I hear footsteps again," he thought, straining to see who was coming. "Thank goodness, a temple worker. Help me, please!" All he could manage was a whisper.

"Wow, you're in pretty bad shape," the temple worker said, "but, I've got to get to work—sorry." He stepped right over the man and kept on walking.

It was nearly dark before the man heard someone else passing by. This time he didn't open his eyes or make a sound. He had given up on anyone helping him. But then, he felt someone gently lift his head and slide a pillow underneath. "This has to be a dream," he thought as he peeked through one eye. "This fellow is a Samaritan—they hate us Jews. Why would he stop to help me?"

Let's hear it for the good Samaritan!

The poor man must have passed out then. But, he woke up
later in a nice clean bed. His cuts were clean and bandaged. The
Samaritan was asking the innkeeper to take care of the hurt
man—he even paid him gold pieces for the man's room and care.
"Well, you never know who your friends really are . . . until you
need them," he thought as he snuggled in to go back to sleep.

Based on Luke 10:30–37

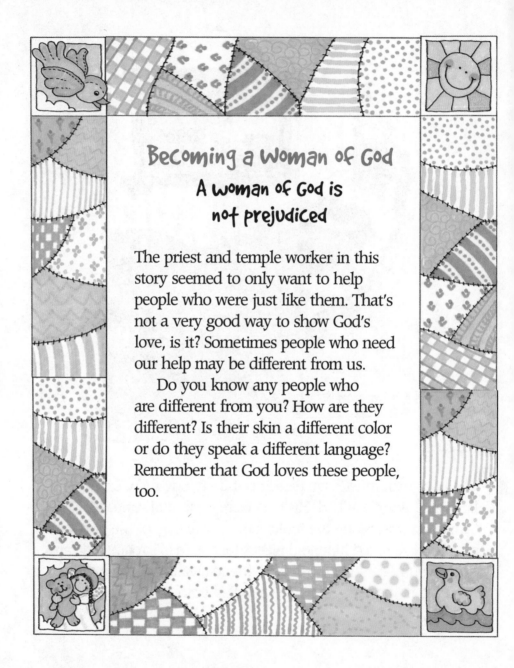

Becoming a Woman of God
A woman of God is not prejudiced

The priest and temple worker in this story seemed to only want to help people who were just like them. That's not a very good way to show God's love, is it? Sometimes people who need our help may be different from us.

Do you know any people who are different from you? How are they different? Is their skin a different color or do they speak a different language? Remember that God loves these people, too.

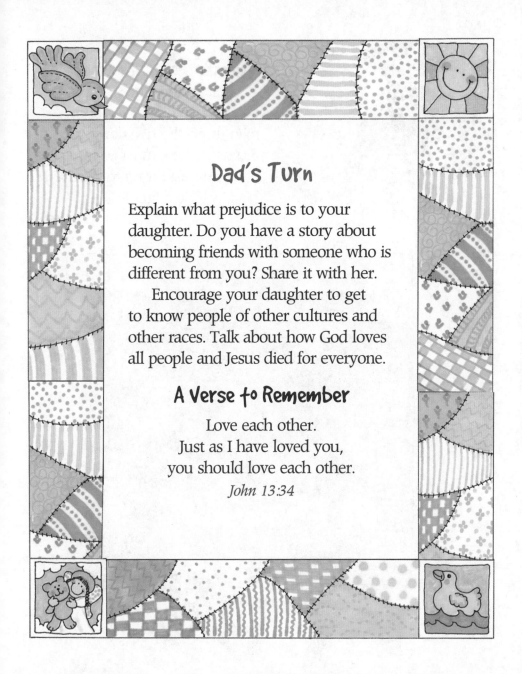

Dad's Turn

Explain what prejudice is to your daughter. Do you have a story about becoming friends with someone who is different from you? Share it with her.

Encourage your daughter to get to know people of other cultures and other races. Talk about how God loves all people and Jesus died for everyone.

A Verse to Remember

Love each other.
Just as I have loved you,
you should love each other.

John 13:34

"Plant the seed . . . hoe the field . . . mend the fences. I can't take it anymore!" The young man threw the hoe down in disgust. "There must be more to life than this. I want to see the big city—live a little!"

The young man ran into the barn shouting, "Hey, Dad, give me my share of your money now. I'm going to get it someday anyway." When his son took the money and headed for the big city, the old man watched sadly.

In the city, the young man was always surrounded by friends who enjoyed helping him spend his money. He loved the fancy clothes and expensive restaurants. But then, he ran out of money . . . and suddenly all his "friends" were gone. The boy was all by himself. Meanwhile, his dad kept watching for him to come home.

"I can't believe that none of my friends would help me. I paid for everything for them—before my money ran out. Now, the only job I can get is feeding these pigs and they have more to eat than I do." Meanwhile, his dad kept watching for him to come home.

As the young man walked home, he came up with a plan. "I'll just ask Dad for a job because I don't deserve to be called his son anymore." When his dad ran out to meet him, he tried to say how sorry he was and that he didn't deserve to be called his son anymore, but his dad hugged him so tight that he couldn't get the words out. What the boy didn't know was that his father had watched and watched for him to come home—never giving up hope!

Based on Luke 15:11–32

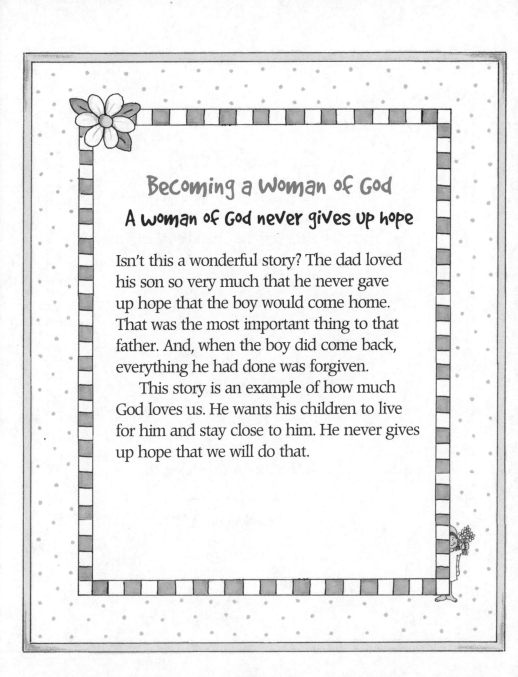

Becoming a Woman of God
A woman of God never gives up hope

Isn't this a wonderful story? The dad loved his son so very much that he never gave up hope that the boy would come home. That was the most important thing to that father. And, when the boy did come back, everything he had done was forgiven.

This story is an example of how much God loves us. He wants his children to live for him and stay close to him. He never gives up hope that we will do that.

Dad's Turn

Share a story with your daughter about a time when you rebelled against your parents. How did they handle it? Did they ever give up hope that you would come back to them? How did you feel when everything worked out and they welcomed you with open arms?

Tell your daughter how much you love her. Assure her that nothing can ever change that love. Remind her of how much God loves her and that he is always waiting for her to come to him.

A Verse to Remember

Love never gives up.
1 Corinthians 13:7

forgotten Thanks

LUKE
17:11-19

"I hate this rotten disease! Having leprosy means I can't even see my family and I lost my job. I have to live in this lousy leper colony. This stinks!" a man shouted, shaking his fist at the sky.

"I know," another man said quietly. "I wish I could just hug my kids."

Jesus and the crowd of people who were always with him passed by the leper colony on their way to Jerusalem. "Jesus, please help us!" someone cried. Jesus looked around and saw ten men standing behind some trees. Their heads and hands were wrapped in strips of cloth—they were lepers. The only part of their faces he could see were their eyes. Eyes filled with hope.

Jesus calmly walked toward the men—even though other people were backing away from the lepers. "Go into town and show yourself to the priest," he told them.

People in the crowd whispered, "Did you hear that? He told them to go into town—they can't go near people—they're lepers! Someone might catch the disease from them!"

Jesus Loves Everyone

KEEP OUT! Lepers

The ten men took off running toward the nearby town. They didn't care what anyone thought, except Jesus! "Hey, you guys, look at my hands. The white leprosy spots are fading!" one man called to the others.

All ten men stopped to check their own hands, arms, and faces—anywhere leprosy had been eating away their skin. "It's gone! My leprosy is gone, too! Jesus healed me! I can go home!" each man shouted.

Nine men took off running for their homes and their families. But, one man didn't even hesitate—he turned right around and went back to Jesus. He dropped to the ground, his face near Jesus' feet. "Thank you, thank you so much for healing me," he whispered through his tears.

"You're welcome," Jesus answered, lifting the man to his feet, "but where are the other nine? Didn't I heal ten men???"

Based on Luke 17:11–19

Becoming a Woman of God
A woman of God says thank you

Jesus healed ten lepers, but only one took the time to say thank you. How do you think that made Jesus feel? When a person does something really nice for someone else, it's nice to hear a thank-you. It makes a person know that what they have done is appreciated.

If a person doesn't remember to say thank you, then people won't want to do nice things for him anymore. Saying "thank you" shows that you know the person made an effort to do something nice for you.

Do you remember to say thank you when someone does something for you? How do you feel when you do something for another person and they don't thank you?

Dad's Turn

Saying thank you is just a nice thing to remember to do. Tell your daughter about a time when someone did a very nice thing for you. Did you remember to thank them? Can you recall a time when you helped someone, and they thanked you? How did you feel? Did you want to do something for that person again?

Make a list together of things God has done for you. Thank him together. Try to remember to thank him for one thing every day.

A Verse to Remember

Give thanks to the LORD and proclaim his greatness. Let the whole world know what he has done.

1 Chronicles 16:8

Keep
ON
Asking!

Luke 18:1-8

"How long are you going to let that guy cheat you?" The woman looked helpless as her mean landlord walked away, counting the money he had just cheated her out of.

"Well?" her neighbor asked again.

"I don't know what to do," she said softly.

"Well, if you don't do something, all the money your dead husband left you will be gone. You've got to stop him," the neighbor said.

She knew that her friend was right. The only thing she could think to do was to see the local judge. He might help her . . . though she had heard that he wasn't a very nice man.

"Get outta my sight. Get lost! You're a bunch of losers who can't settle your own family problems!" This judge had forgotten that he was supposed to help people. Most people wondered why he became a judge—he didn't even seem to like people.

"Gulp." The woman took a deep breath before marching up to the judge. "Will you please stop my landlord from cheating me? I'm a widow and I don't have much money," she explained. The judge turned his dark, angry eyes on her and stared for a few minutes.

"Get out of here. I can't be bothered with such piddly problems," he growled.

Sadly turning to leave, the woman was ready to give up easily. *Wait a minute; what do I have to lose?* she thought. *If he doesn't help me I'm going to lose everything anyway.* So she marched right back to the judge. "Sir, you are the only one who can help me. Please listen to my story." She almost fainted when the judge shouted, "I said to get out of here!"

But the little woman was not one to give up easily. Time after time she went back to the judge and respectfully asked him to help her with her problem. Time after time, he sent her away. But, every time he looked up, there she was again. Finally he sighed, "You're wearing me out. I'm going to see that you get the help you need because you just keep asking me."

Based on Luke 18:1–8

Becoming a Woman of God
A Woman of God is persistent in prayer

The little lady could have just asked the judge for help one time, then given up. The judge wasn't very nice, so it was probably hard for her to keep going back to him. But, what she wanted was important to her, so she kept asking and kept asking. Finally, the judge got tired of her bothering him, so he gave her what she wanted.

When you want something from your mom or dad, do you just ask once then give up? If it is something you really want, you ask over and over again, don't you? Sometimes that works and you get what you want, and sometimes it doesn't. But, when you keep asking, your parents know that it is important to you.

Dad's Turn

Tell your daughter about something you really wanted when you were a young boy. Explain to her how you asked your parents repeatedly for that thing. Did you finally get it or did you eventually give up?

The Bible tells us to keep asking God when we want him to do something for us. Ask over and over again and don't give up. We won't talk him into doing something he doesn't want to do, but he will know how important that thing is to us.

A Verse to Remember

Keep on asking,
and you will be given what you ask for.
Keep on looking, and you will find.
Keep on knocking, and the door will be opened.

Matthew 7:7

BIRD'S EYE VIEW

ACTS 3:1-10

"Outta my way, scum—I said MOVE IT! Don't you know who I am? Let me through . . . I order you to get outta the way!" For once in his life, no one paid any attention to the tough little man.

Crowds of people swarmed the streets, and a tax collector like
Zacchaeus, who cheated and overcharged people, had no chance
of anyone letting him move to the front. Everyone wanted to see
Jesus. The famous teacher taught about God, healed sick people,
and raised the dead back to life.

Meanwhile, little Zacchaeus had an idea. A big sycamore tree grew back off the road a bit. One of its branches hung out over the crowd of people. So, Zacchaeus shinnied up the tree and scooted out to the end of the branch. Now, he was hanging right over the road where Jesus would pass.

A few minutes later Jesus and a crowd of people appeared down the road. As they moved toward the crowd around the tree, cries of "Jesus, look at me"; "Jesus, over here; heal my friend . . . come to my house," filled the air. Zacchaeus just sat quietly on his tree branch and watched the whole thing.

As Jesus passed under the tree branch, he looked up at Zacchaeus. "Come on down, Zacchaeus. I want to come to your house today."

Why would Jesus go to a tax collector's house? people wondered.

But, after Zacchaeus talked with Jesus for a while, he knew it had been wrong to cheat people. The little tax collector promised Jesus to pay back everyone he had cheated—four times more than he had cheated them!

Based on Luke 19:1–10

Becoming a Woman of God

A Woman of God Changes when She Meets Jesus

Zacchaeus wasn't a nice person. He cheated others and he thought he was more important than the regular people. So, he didn't have many friends, and no one wanted to help him when he needed help. He must have been pretty lonely. But, when Jesus talked to him and told him about God's love, Zacchaeus changed. He was sorry for the way he had cheated people and he wanted to change. That must have been hard for people to believe, but that is the effect Jesus had on people.

Have you ever treated someone badly? When you think about how Jesus wants you to treat others are you sorry for being mean or unfair to someone else?

Dad's Turn

Tell your daughter about some change in your life. Did you have a bad habit that you worked to overcome? Did your lifestyle change when you met Jesus? Talk about how it is important to live your life as a good example of who Jesus is.

Remind your daughter that some people may not go to church, but if they know that we are Christians, they will watch how we treat others and decide what God's love is like by how we live.

Ask your daughter if she thinks she needs to make any changes in the way she treats others.

A Verse to Remember

For God so loved the world
that he gave his only Son,
so that everyone who believes in him
will not perish but have eternal life.

John 3:16

"Come on, John, it's almost 3:00. The prayer service will be starting soon." John gulped down the rest of his lunch and wiped his mouth with his hand as he followed Peter out the door. The temple wasn't far away, but the streets were crowded with people.

WHAT COULD BE BETTER than MONEY?

ACTS 3:1-10

"Excuse us, coming through!" Some men were trying to get through the crowd. They were carrying a man who couldn't walk.

"They bring that guy here every day to beg for money," Peter observed. He and John watched as the man settled down near the temple gate and started begging from anyone entering the temple.

Peter slowly walked over to the crippled man and just stood in front of him. The man held up his cup, expecting Peter to drop some money in it. "I don't have any money," Peter said quietly.

"Then get out of the way," the man said in disgust. He turned to catch other people going through the gate.

"Look at me," Peter quietly ordered. "I have something better for you than money." The man didn't look so sure—what could be better than money?

"Come on, we're going to be late for prayers." John tugged at Peter's sleeve, but Peter shook him away and turned back to the man.

"In the name of Jesus, GET UP AND WALK," he said.

Peter took the man's hand and helped him to his feet. At first
the man didn't understand what had happened—his feet and legs
were healed! Carefully trying his new legs, he took a step, then
a hop; finally he was jumping and shouting, "I'm healed! I'm
healed! Praise God for the gift that is better than money!"

Based on Acts 3:1–10

Becoming a Woman of God
A Woman of God gives the best gifts

The crippled man thought that the best gift he could get was money. But, Peter knew better. He knew that God would help him heal the man. He was willing to interrupt his schedule, be late for the prayer service, in order to help the crippled man.

Have you ever been able to help someone? How did it feel to help someone else? Did it interrupt your schedule or what you were doing? Did you mind?

Dad's Turn

What is the best gift you ever received? Why was it so special? Who gave it to you? What's the best gift you've ever given your daughter? Why did you enjoy giving it so much? Did you ever feel like your schedule was being interrupted in order to give this gift?

Talk about the best gift God has given— salvation through believing in Jesus Christ. Aren't you glad that Jesus didn't worry about his schedule being interrupted? Thank him for his gift of love.

A Verse to Remember

The free gift of God is eternal life through Jesus Christ our Lord.

Romans 6:23

Yours, Mine, and Ours

"Why do we always have to meet secretly? Why can't we just sit outside and sing praise to God like we used to?" a young man wondered out loud. Life had not been easy since Jesus was murdered. Some people thought the Christians had stolen his body so it would look like he came back to life. Some people made life really hard for the Christians.

"Don't get discouraged. It's important for us to hang together. We all miss Jesus. We're all confused about what has happened. But, we have to stick together." The disciples stepped up to be leaders of the group of Christians after Jesus left.

"Well, that's easy for you to say. Since I lost my job, my kids are hungry." The young man was really worried. "I'm sorry, I know that God will take care of us. It's just hard sometimes," he whispered.

Barnabas stepped up to the young man and put his arms around the man. "The most important thing for us to do is tell others about Jesus' love. We must be able to tell people that Jesus died because he loves them and that he came back to life and lives in heaven today. You can't do that if you're hungry or worried. Here, I sold some of my land and I want you to have this money."

"I have extra flour and oil," one old woman said. "If anyone needs some to make bread for your family, come see me."

Another man mentioned that he had cows who gave good milk. A young woman had chickens who laid lots of eggs. Everyone started looking for ways they could help one another.

No one in the little church went hungry or had unpaid bills. If one person needed money, someone else sold a field and donated the money. If someone needed help, people volunteered to do what they could. All the time, the Christians shared God's love with others. People in the town could see how much they cared for each other. The Christians were good examples of God's love.

Based on Acts 4:32–37

Becoming a Woman of God
A woman of God shares

The Christians in this early church took care of one another. If one was hungry or didn't have clothes or a place to live, another man sold some land and gave the money to his needy friend. That's the way we should help one another today.

If you have two blankets and someone else doesn't have any, should you put your extra blanket in a closet, or give it to the other person? Has another person shared something with you? Have you been able to share with another person?

Dad's Turn

Tell your daughter about a time when someone shared something with you. How did you feel about it? How did you feel about that person? Now tell her about a time when you shared with someone. Did you feel good about it? Did the person appreciate what you shared?

Talk about ways you can share what you have with those who are less fortunate. Come up with a plan to work in an inner city neighborhood, or support a child overseas, or give your old clothing to a mission. Find some way you and your daughter can share together.

A Verse to Remember

Blessed are those who are generous.

Proverbs 22:9

Singin', Shakin', and Savin'

"Toss 'em in jail and throw away the key!" "Yeah, the bums are just troublemakers!" Before Paul and Silas could answer, sticks were ripping through the air, hitting them and pounding them until they could barely stand. Then they were dragged away to prison.

"You won't escape from here." The jailer pushed Paul and Silas to the floor in the smallest cell, tucked away in the very center of the jail. No windows—no chance to even see daylight or breathe fresh air—and no chance for escape or rescue! He roughly clamped their feet into stocks. "You can rot here for all I care," he spat at them.

God will help you...

As soon as they could breathe normally, Paul and Silas started praying and singing praises to God. "What you got to sing about— haven't you noticed that you're in prison or that you've been beaten bloody?" The other prisoners made fun of Paul and Silas.

By midnight, the other prisoners seemed to be comforted by Paul and Silas's singing. They were quiet, listening to the gentle praises. It was about midnight when the floor began to shake. Pieces of the ceiling cracked and dropped down on the prisoners. As the doors broke off and chains popped like paper, men shouted, "We're free! Run!"

But Paul didn't let anyone leave. When the jailer ran in and saw the doors were broken off, he cried, "My prisoners—they've all escaped!" He drew his sword to kill himself.

"Stop! We're all here," Paul shouted. The jailer couldn't believe that Paul had kept all the prisoners in the jail.

"Can you tell me how to be a Christian like you?" he asked. Paul was very happy to do just that!

Based on Acts 16:16–34

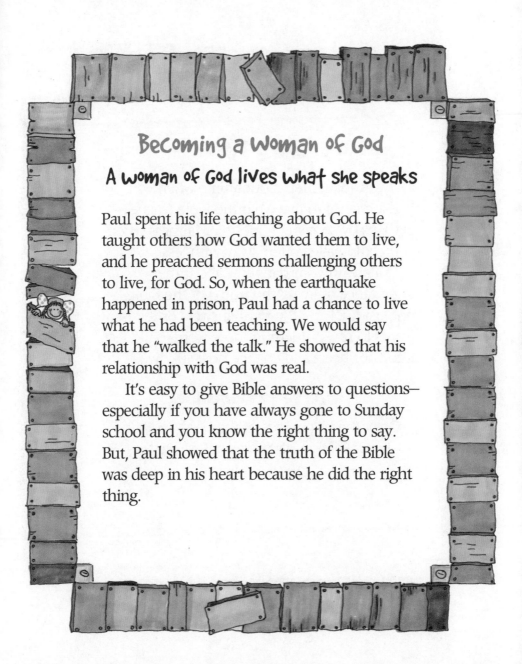

Becoming a Woman of God
A woman of God lives what she speaks

Paul spent his life teaching about God. He taught others how God wanted them to live, and he preached sermons challenging others to live, for God. So, when the earthquake happened in prison, Paul had a chance to live what he had been teaching. We would say that he "walked the talk." He showed that his relationship with God was real.

It's easy to give Bible answers to questions—especially if you have always gone to Sunday school and you know the right thing to say. But, Paul showed that the truth of the Bible was deep in his heart because he did the right thing.

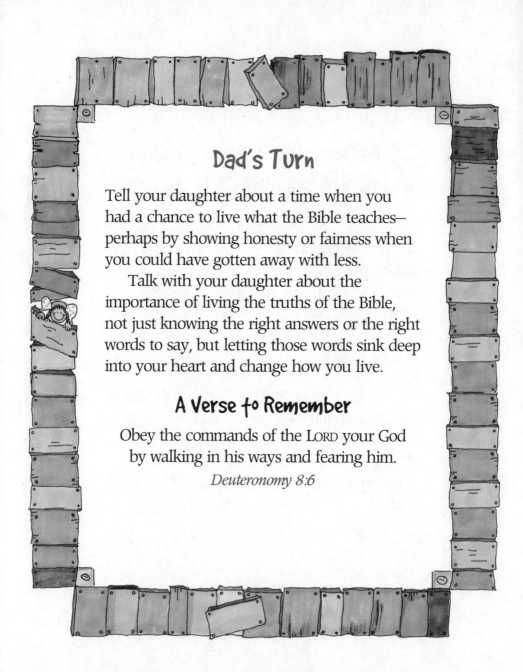

Dad's Turn

Tell your daughter about a time when you had a chance to live what the Bible teaches—perhaps by showing honesty or fairness when you could have gotten away with less.

Talk with your daughter about the importance of living the truths of the Bible, not just knowing the right answers or the right words to say, but letting those words sink deep into your heart and change how you live.

A Verse to Remember

Obey the commands of the LORD your God by walking in his ways and fearing him.

Deuteronomy 8:6

Eavesdropping

"Uncle Paul, I'm scared. Why did those men put you in prison?" Paul's young nephew visited him at the jail every day.

"They're angry because I teach about God," Paul answered. That confused the boy even more—the men who put him in prison were teachers in the temple. Why should they be angry that Paul taught about God? "It will be OK. Go on home and get some rest," Paul encouraged his young nephew.

In their regular farewell ritual, the boy stuck his hand between the prison bars. Paul grasped the small hand between his own hands for just a second. Then the boy started home. As he rounded a corner he could hear men's voices coming through an open window. They sounded angry. He quietly slipped against the wall and listened for a few minutes. He couldn't believe what he heard!

Racing back to the prison, he called, as loudly as he dared, "Uncle Paul, Uncle Paul! Some men are going to hurt you. They're going to trick the commander into bringing you to the High Council for questioning. Only, they're going to kidnap you and kill you!"

"Shhhh, keep your voice down," Paul cautioned. "Are you sure about this?" he whispered.

When the young boy nodded his head, Paul continued. "OK, here's what you've got to do. I'll call the main officer over here and you tell him what you just told me. You are sure, aren't you?"

"Yeah, the men even promised each other that they wouldn't eat anything until you're dead!" The boy's eyes were as big as saucers. He was worried about his uncle's safety.

The brave young man did exactly what Paul told him to do. Quickly the officer arranged for 200 soldiers, 200 spearmen, and 70 horsemen to get Paul safely out of town. Paul gave his nephew a big hug before leaving. "You saved my life. I don't know when I'll see you again, but I'll never forget this," he told the boy.

Based on Acts 23:12–35

Becoming a Woman of God
A Woman of God tells an adult

Paul's nephew saved Paul's life. When he heard the bad thing that the men were planning, he told Paul about it. That took courage, didn't it? Paul knew exactly what to do.

Sometimes we may know when there is a problem, but we don't know what to do about it. It's a good idea to tell someone you can trust who is older and wiser.

Have you ever told an adult about some problem you have or that you have heard about? How did it work out? How did the adult help you?

Dad's Turn

If you have a story about confiding in an adult or seeking an adult's help when you were a child, share that story with your daughter. Perhaps there was a time when you should have sought an adult's help and you didn't. Tell her how that situation turned out.

If your daughter has ever confided a problem to you, compliment her on remembering to do that. Talk with her about what kinds of things she might want to talk to an adult about. Help her think of other adults she can trust.

A Verse to Remember

Teach your children to
choose the right path,
and when they are older,
they will remain upon it.
Proverbs 22:6

Carolyn Larsen has written more than thirty books for children and adults. She is a frequent conference speaker around the world, bringing scriptural messages filled with humor and tenderness. She is also active in a theater troupe and cofounded the group Flashpoints, which uses drama and creative movement to minister at women's events.

Caron Turk is an artist whose work has appeared in the bestselling series of Little Boys/Little Girls Storybooks as well as in numerous original paintings, designs, and stamps.

Bible stories for
mothers & sons ...

In *Little Boys Bible Storybook for Mothers and Sons*, all stories are uniquely told from a mother's perspective. Includes additional material not found in *Little Boys Bible Storybook*.

... and **fathers & sons** to read together.

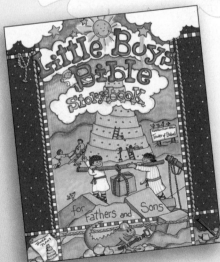

In *Little Boys Bible Storybook for Fathers and Sons*, all stories are uniquely told from a father's perspective. Includes additional material not found in *Little Boys Bible Storybook*.

Bible stories for
mothers & daughters ...

In *Little Girls Bible Storybook for Mothers and Daughters*, all stories are uniquely told from a mother's perspective. Includes additional material not found in *Little Girls Bible Storybook*.

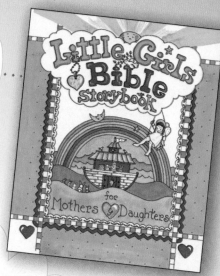

... and **fathers & daughters** to read together.

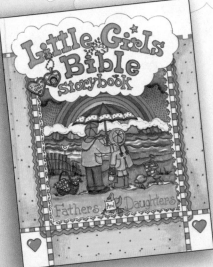

In *Little Girls Bible Storybook for Fathers and Daughters*, all stories are uniquely told from a father's perspective. Includes additional material not found in *Little Girls Bible Storybook*.

BakerBooks

Relevant. Intelligent. Engaging.

www.bakerbooks.com